AUDIO-VISUAL AIDS TO EDUCATIONAL TECHNOLOGY

AUDIO-VISUAL AIDS TO EDUCATIONAL TECHNOLOGY

Prof. Harmesh Lal

Co-authors

Dr. Shailendra Bhushan

Dr. Meenu Kumar

Ocean Books Pvt. Ltd.

ISO 9001:2015 Publishers

Published by
Ocean Books (P) Ltd.
4/19 Asaf Ali Road,
New Delhi-110 002 (INDIA)
e-mail: info@oceanbooks.in

ISBN 978-81-8430-543-2
Audio-Visual Aids to Educational Technology
by Prof. Harmesh Lal
Dr. Shailendra Bhushan
Dr. Meenu Kumar

Edition
2025

Price
₹ 500.00 (Rupees Five Hundred only)

Printed at
R-Tech Offset Printers, Delhi

**JANARDAN RAI NAGAR
RAJASTHAN VIDYAPEETH (DEEMED-TO-BE) UNIVERSITY**
**(NAAC Accredited 'A' Grade University)
Pratap Nagar, Udaipur 313001**

Prof. S.S. Sarangdevot
Vice Chancellor

FOREWORD

The use of technological aids and devices goes back to 1948, immediately after the independence when the audio-visual scheme was included in the educational development plan with the limited objectives of promoting the use of educational films and radio broadcasting in addition to the other projected and non-projected aids with the Central Film Library as its nucleus. An important beginning was made in 1971-72 with the development of Educational Technology project as a new scheme in the fourth Five Year Plan which was intended to stimulate the use of Television as well as instructional media to improve the quality of education with the objective of creating an infrastructure necessary for the use of TV facilities for education which were made available under the Satellite Instructional Television Experiment (SITE) involving collaboration on a systematic basis between the media agencies and the educational institutions in the planning, production and use of media programmes. It was a unique experiment in the realm of education and communication, not only in India but perhaps in the whole world.

The overall objective was to improve the quality of education at all levels to reduce stagnation and wastage extending the benefits of technology to large groups especially in rural areas. The scheme was centrally sponsored and envisaged by setting up of three agencies, viz., ET Unit in the Ministry of Human Resource Development (Earlier Ministry of Education) for policy formulation, coordination and for provision of finance; Centre for Educational Technology in the NCERT and ET cells in the State Departments of Education for promoting the use of Educational Technology. Later, in 1984, the Department of Teaching Aids and the Centre for Educational Technology were merged and the Institute known as Central Institute of Educational Technology was set up under the umbrella of NCERT.

With the launching of Satellite in 1975-76, Instructional TV programmes were transmitted directly from the Satellite to reception TV sets in the rural areas, covering 2,330 villages in widely separated clusters in 6 States. TV sets were placed mostly in primary schools and Panchayat Ghars. State Educational Technology cells were made responsible for ensuring the proper use of Mass Media.

Educational Technology with great potential of using Mass Media for education has made rapid strides to promote universalisation of elementary education and adult education. Dr. Harmesh Lal, Professor, ET has worked in the media institute of NCERT (known as the National Institute of Audio Visual Education, department of Teaching Aids and the Central Institute of Educational Technology). He has written large number of papers on Media and Technology, which have been published in National/International Journals.

Professor Lal has also produced more than 100 ETV, Radio programmes, some of which have won awards in the national and the international competitions. Full-fledged chapter on Low Cost Technological Aids has been devoted in the book which is very close to the reality of the practices presently prevailing in the large number of rural/backward areas.

The present book authored by him 'From Audio-Visual Aids to Educational Technology' depicts the wide range of projects and programmes on educational technology which would be very helpful to the teachers and teacher educators for enriching their experiences in improving the teaching learning process. It is hoped that the book shall be found useful in enhancing the. professional and academic advancement of students, teachers and teacher-educators, especially those aspiring for pursuing courses in Diploma in Elementary Education, B.Ed. and MA in Education/M.Ed., etc.

(Professor S.S. Sarangdevot)

PREFACE

Having worked for more than 37 years is educational media, it gives me a great pleasure, to be in close association with thousands of students, teachers and teacher educators across the country especially with the rural education workers NGO's involved in teaching-learning situations such as Social Work and Research Centre, Tilonia (Rajasthan), Mitraniketan in Vellanad Thiruvantapuram (Kerala) Kishore Bharti in Palia Piperia village, Bankhedi block (Hoshangabad Distt) and Vikram Sarabhai Community Science Centre Ahemdabad etc. The innovative work in the field of Education, being done by the above mentioned centres in close collaboration with the Govt. Departments and educational institutions inspired me to undertake the task of synthesizing the experiences gained in the field of education. An attempt has been made to highlight the preparation of teaching-learning aids, with the help of locally available material by involving the teachers, students and the artisans. Our schools suffer heavily due to the shortage of funds and the emphasis on the use of environmental material to fabricate the technological aids, serves the dual purpose viz., preparation and use of aids from the material, available locally at low cost/ no cost and at the same time the schools are likely to use such aids with confidence as they are part and parcel of the preparation process.

There are certain concepts involving motion which are difficult to transact without the help of relevant audio-visual aids. In such situations we can make use of Audio, Television, Films and Computer Aided programs. The marriage of television with the computer for animated experiments and for better comprehension of concepts can help immensely to solve our conceptual problems which are otherwise difficult to comprehend. Audio-Visual programmes can be prepared or procured from the National agencies such as NCERT and Consortium for Educational Communication (CEC) etc.

With the advent of Information and Communication Technology (ICT) and the resultant Technological growth, new methods and materials/

resources are being harnessed both at the formal as well as non-formal levels of education. Many abstract concepts can be easily grasped with simple technological aids for profound creative thought which not only provide enrichment for preparatory exercise but are also used as play way materials and models in some form or the other.

I am highly thankful to Professor S.S. Sarang devot, Vice-chancellor Rajasthan, Vidyapeeth (Deemed to be) University (NAAC Accredited A. grade) Udaipur for sparing his valuable time from his busy schedule in writing the 'Foreword' of the book which encouraged me to accomplish the task of writing the chapters expeditiously.

Thanks are due to Shri Piyush ji of Prabhat Publications (Ocean Books Pvt. Ltd) and the entire concerned staff for finalizing the format of the manuscript and bringing out the book in its present form. I also thanks Shri Manoj Gupta of M/S. Prabhat Publications for finalizing the cover page and for editing the content matter of the book. Last but not the least I am extremely thankful to my old colleague Dr. Shailender Bhushan who gave me the encouragement to write the manuscript which was a gigantic task.

HARMESH LAL
Formerly Professor, Educational
Technology, NCERT, N.Delhi 110016

CONTENTS

1

AUDIO-VISUAL AIDS—HISTORICAL PERSPECTIVE

Learners receive information mainly through audio-visual aids. During the last few decades, the emphasis has been on teaching rather than learning in the teaching-learning precess. Besides audio-visual aids we can include the aids which communicate through touch and skills such as models, feelings or simulators and other devices which have been in use in education since very ancient times.

Immediately after the independence an audio-visual education section consisting 4-5 persons was set up by the then Ministry of Education which conducted all the activities in this field, with Central Film Library as its nucleus. Gradually, audio-visual education units were set up in the states which were being coordinated by the Central Govt., Ministry of Education, New Delhi.

The National Institute of Audio-Visual Education (NIAVE) was set up in 1959 by the Govt. of India, with Shri G.K. Athalye as its Director. In 1961, the NIAVE was merged with the National Council of Education Research and Training (NCERT) as a Department of the National Institute of Education.

NIAVE was primarily concerned with the development of instructional materials for the school curriculum and was involved in providing training in the theory, preparation and utilization of audio-visual materials to the teachers, teacher-educators and other groups working in the field of education.

NIAVE provided leadership in the field of audio-visual education by organizing seminars, workshops, study groups and conferences in the country.

Audio-visual education involves the use of instructional devices such as motion pictures, film trips, television recordings, graphic illustrations like charts maps, models, dioramas, demonstrations etc. Such devices popularly known as audio-visual aids, transmit ideas and experiences through eyes and ears. They emphasize the use of concrete or non-verbal experience in the learning process. Other forms of instruction stress verbal or symbolic experience.

The basic element of the visual aids is their pictorial content. They present the subject matter mainly through the medium of pictures and sketches. They facilitate the formation of mental images which are so basic to learning.

A broad background and perceptual experience is the basis for learning as our senses provide stimuli for our perceptual reorganization. Sometimes these materials of instruction that are less abstract than words, are known as multi-sensory materials.

Classification of Audio-Visual Aids

(A) Graphics Aids

(1) Photographs and Pictures
(2) Flash cards and strips
(3) Posters
(4) Charts
(5) Diagrams
(6) Graphs
(7) Maps
(8) Cartoons
(9) Comics
(10)Print Materials

(b) Display Boards

(1) Black/chalk Boards
(2) Flannel Boards
(3) Bulletin Boards
(4) Magnetic Boards
(5) Peg Boards

(c) Three Dimensional Aids

(1) Models
(2) Objects

(D) Projected Aids

(1) Films
(2) Filmstrip

(3) Specimens	(3) Slides
(4) Mock ups	(4) T.V. programs
(5) Dioramas	(5) Computer Aided Instruction
(6) Puppets	
(E) Audio Aids	**(F) Activities**
(1) Radio	(1) Field Trips
(2) Television	(2) Dermonstrations
(3) Recordings	(3) Dramatics

(A) GRAPHIC AIDS

Graphics are instructional rnaterials that visualize and simplify ideas and facts. They convey meaning mainly through relatively conventionalized syrnbols that are nearer to reality perceptually than verbal syrnbols, and relatively farther from reality perceptually than pictures. Graphics catch and hold our attention through symbolic representations to clarify ideas-and to highlight the rnain points of a topic. They represent the subject-matter in a condensed and understandable form. Graphics, in the professional language, indicate materials which illustrate ideas, objects, concepts and processes boldly, clearly and vigorously through a synthesis of drawings, pictures and words.

(B) DISPLAY BOARDS

Display boards are devices that exhibit graphic and allied materials for learning. Generally, they display visual materials on correlated topics.

(C) THREE-DIMENSIONAL AIDS

They represent materials that are not flat like graphic aids but are vivid and realistic representations of reality. They give the concrete experience in learning. They provide either real, or modified sensory experiences when they represent actual objects or models.

(D) PROJECTED AIDS

They constitute a wide range of teaching aids from the projected illustrations to the television. They compress ideas and information that are represented graphically and forcefully through successive frames. Projected aids minimise the chances of distraction in a darkroom.

(E) AUDIO AIDS

These are materials which are the sources of audio learning experiences. These are radio and recordings of radio broadcasts, and tape recordings of educational programmes. The television and the film, which are audio-visual materials, too have an effective audio part.

(F) ACTIVITY AIDS

These are such activities that provide learning experiences. They develop direct purposeful situations for learning.

Graphics as Basic Visual Materials

Graphics are a powerful medium for teaching and learning. In some or other they are represented in most instructional materials. Graphic materials possess all these characteristics. These are effective instructional materials.

Graphics develop a forceful shorthand language. Their basic functions are to attract attention, convey meaning clearly and facilitate learning. They make an impact on the reader. They have universal appeal and their educational values are manifold.

Graphic materials are usually two-dimensional representations. Many of these can be projected through an opaque projector or from films, filmstrips and slides. They can take the form of dynamic illustrations on flannel boards, chalk boards and other display boards.

Specific Advantages of Audio-Visual Aids

1. Help students learn more-
   Proved by research studies.
2. Help them remember longer -
   Build more permanent learning in every curricular area.
3. Provide effective stimulus to learning -
   Involve the students by absorbing devices.
4. Make learning more concrete
   Give meaning to the printed word.
5. Bring the world into the classroom.
   Schools can no longer be isolated from life.

6. Provide a variety of approaches to the same subject
   Constant use of the same medium and technique is boring for the learners.

Effective Use of Audio-Visual Aids

Adds interest and involvement

Makes learning permanent

Reduces verbalism

Develops greater understanding

Removes the barriers of classroom walls

Stimulates self-activity

Fosters continuity of thought

Helps us in overcoming language barriers

Takes the message to many people

Provides a great variety of methods

Makes teaching-learning effeciently

Brings the world into the classroom

The Central Film Library is the largest library of educational film in the whole of South East Asia. It has 5700 instructional films and nearly 2000 filmstrips in its stock which are all in a state of decay although a few films have been transferred on T.V. cassettes/CD s.

A variety of training and extension programs and activities were being organized by the institution in the preparation and use of audio-visual aids in order to disseminate ideas and techniques of A.V. instruction. NIAVE has also been conducting research and evaluation of the efficacy of A.V. materials.

Later on as per decision taken at the highest level, all the institutes of the NCERT at the headquarters were converted into departments in mid-sixties with the exception of Central Institute of Education which became a part of Delhi University, Delhi. National Institute of Audio-Visual Education was converted into the Department of Audio-Visual Education and then into the Department of Teaching Aids with the same functions and activities which were being undertaken by the NIAVE.

With the advent of Educational Technology in India in early seventies, a Centre for Educational Technology was set up by the Ministry of Education, Govt. of India in the NCERT and subsequently Educational Technology Units were set up in the states. Side by side the university Departments prescribed Education Technology a unit in the method of teaching or an optional paper at the Diploma in Education, B.Ed./M.Ed./ M.A. in Education or even at the Ph.D. level. Some of the universities even offer Education Technology as a compulsory paper or as an important unit in the method of teaching.

When Educational Technology came to India, it was taken as an imported luxury from the West. Even the teachers/teacher educators questioned its utility stating that the Educational Technology does not contribute to the teaching-learning process. But its contribution has changed the outlook of the teachers, students and the educators which shall be elaborated later as to how educational technology can promote and enhance educational opportunities, equity and improve the quality of educational processes at all levels of education.

Central Institute of Educational Technology (CIET), a constitutent wing of the NCERT was set up by the Govt. of India in 1984 with the merger of Centre for Educational Technology and the Department of Teaching Aids. CIET symbolizes the development of Educational Technology at the national level. Its major aim is to create an awareness about the use of Educational Technology and to promote the utilization of modern techniques, infrastructure and facilities such as educational audio-radio, television, computer aided instruction, graphics, low cost aids, satellite communication and cyber media, etc. The main areas of activities and functions are to:

- Design and develop media software.
- Undertake research and evaluation studies or Educational Technology.
- Design and develop technological aids.
- Disseminate media programs for broadcast and non-broadcast modes.
- Organize training programs for capacity building in various aspects of Educational Technology.
- Advise and coordinate academic and technical programs of the State Institutes of Educational Technology (SIETS) set up by the Ministry of Human Resource Development.

- Document media programs for dissemination and utilization.
- Provide consultancy in the development, evaluation and utilization.

Since its inception, the CIET has been feeding regular services of educational TV and audio-radio programs for the children of primary, secondary classes and also for the teachers. These programs were being telecast/broadcast through DD-1 on National Network, DD Bharti and through dedicated education channel Gyan Darshan and audio programs through Gyan Vani. However, since 2014 the transmission of video programmes has been stopped on Gyan Darshan. The programs produced by the CIET/SIETs and UGC country wide classroom are available through Open Education Resources, Internet and can be freely accessed by the audience targetted for non-commercial purposes.

CIET is South-East Asia Centre for NHK Japan video library and receives CDs/cassettes of all the NHK Award winning programs which are used by the CIET and the SIETs for reference purposes. Selected programs (both audio, video) are disseminated through non-broadcast mode. It has a sales counter for this purpose. Besides CIET organizes All India Festival of Children. Educational Audio-Video programs for which the entries are invited from all the educational media programe producers/ organizations and the children who produce these programs.

□

2

EDUCATIONAL TECHNOLOGY THE CONCEPT

Educational Technology has its origin since the dawn of independence when Audio-Visual Education units were set up in the states with the educational film libraries, technological aids and graphic sections as important wings during the first five-year plan. It was stressed that audio-visual materials, methods and techniques provide the fundamental means of organizing and revitalizing the curriculum.

New developments in educational media and techniques took place in early seventies with the emergence of educational technology to meet the challenge of achieving the universalization of elementary education. Educational Technology Bureau was established in the Ministry of Human Resource Development under the Educational Technology Scheme of the Govt. of India and State Institutes of Educational Technology were established in the states of Andhra Pradesh, Bihar, Gujarat, Maharashtra, Odisha and U.P. 7th SIET was set up later in the mid-nineties in the Kerala state. The main function of the SIETs was to produce Educational T.V. and audio-radio programs for transmission/broadcast on DD-1 and AIR Stations.

Meaning of Educational Technology

During the process of formal instruction, it is difficult to bring all the necessary experiences and formal education is mainly confined to abstract forms of real experiences. This is more so in the case of concepts which involve motion. It is very difficult to teach such concepts through the books which are static. Such concepts can best be explained through the working models, films, T.V., demonstration or computer-aided instructions. When the technology advanced, the Computer and films made their entry into the educational system in a way which provided the ability to the user to communicate to the medium and to respond to the user. The latest in the arena of educational technology is the Internet technology which connects the entire world. This has resulted improved student performance, enhanced interest in learning, greater retention power, etc.

Theories of learning are changing into the theory of instruction and with research inputs on the process of learning, more novel and rigorous criteria of assessments are being evolved.

Oxford Dictionary meaning of Education is :

The process of learning, growing up;
The process of rearing or bringing up;

It is concerned with teaching-learning and providing systematic instruction for the growth of an individual.

Technology means
Systematic treatment,
Scientific study of practical arts, and :

The process of development of materials and systematic are common. It applies to education and in other cases to materials also.

According to B Erikson, Educational Technology is concerned with each and every aspect of education including:

The psychology of learning
Audio and visual methods of presentation
Educational planning and organisation
Curriculum development and course design
Production of teaching-learning materials
Storage, retrieval and dissemination of information
Allocation of resources
Cost and effectiveness of media in education and problems of innovation

There are numerous definitions of technology. The most accepted one is the systematic application of scientific knowledge to achieve a particular practical purpose, such as systematic design and construction of buildings which can be improved and devised. Educational Technology is used to describe the application of hardware such as computers, filmstrip projector, tape recorders. Such a hardware concept of educational Technology is limited than the application of knowledge to the systematic design of education viz. software part which is Technology of Education. Hardware aspect is Technology in Education. Software includes filmships slides, CDs etc.

Thus, we can say that Educational Technology means anything or everything which enhances the process of teaching learning.

Dr. K. Gopalan, former Director, NCERT defined Educational Technology as the amalgamation of technology in and of education. This covers the presentation of information through hardware and software as well as several aspects such as learner characteristics, the subject matter as well as the application of appropriate principles of various sciences. The definition of the US Commission of Instructional Technology is the most comprehensive which says "Educational Technology is the systematic way of designing, implementing and evaluating the total process of learning and teaching in terms of specific objectives, based on research in human learning and communication and employing a combination of human and non-human resources".

According to G.O.M. Leith, "Educational Technology is the application of scientific knowledge about learning and the conditions of learning to improve the effectiveness and efficiency of teaching and learning". Dr. S.S. Kulkarni defined Edl. Technology "as the application of laws as well as discoveries of science and technology of sciences to the process of education".

Another former Director NCERT, Dr. Shib K. Mitra states "Educational Technology can be conceived as application of scientific rules by methods and materials through which educational goals can be realized."

The development of Educational Technology has four important phases, viz. (i) audio-visual phase, (ii) cybernetic phase, (iii) psychological and sociological phase and; (iv) telecommunication phase.

1. Audio-Visual Phase: This phase represents our old education which had been prevailing since ancient times. Gurus or teachers used to teach their shishyas/students mainly through their voice and gestures.

Slowly and gradually graphics media started making their headway and charts, posters, models, etc. made with the easily available or inexpensive material were used for instructional purposes. In this phase, the teachers used to organize the learning experiences which did not strictly follow the psychological principles of teaching-learning. Teachers hardly took any pre-service teacher training before entering the teaching profession. Old techniques and methods of teaching were in vogue in the teaching-learning process. There was main emphasis of teaching rather than learning. Education was not child-centered and was mainly in the form of one-way communication such as

Teacher—Media—Student.

2. Cybernetic Phase: After the Second World War, education became the prime focus of society and a system of feedback was injected to know the impact of education, imparted to the students and the resultant changes which could be incorporated in teaching-learning. Lot of attention was devoted to the extent of learning as a result of teaching.

This was in the form of:

INPUT ↓ PROCESS ↓ OUTPUT

o

FEED-BACK ↑ COMPARISON-RESULT
TO PROVIDE
REMEDIES

Cybernetic provides for combination of human knowledge, methods/ techniques and all the resources to improve the system for the welfare of human beings.

3. Psychological-Sociological Phase: In this phase psychological and sociological principles are adopted in education processes. This phase has brought a revolution in education. Earlier the questions were being raised as Education for what? B.F. Skinner, and others contributed and invented new psychological and sociological principles, methods and techniques in teaching-learning which perfectly answers education for what?

4. Telecommunication Phase: Telecommunication phase is the present phase of educational technology in which not only the graphics media but also the electronic media with all the modern technologies such as TV, teleconferencing, computers, mobile phones are being harnessed in the service of education, both for teaching and learning. Internet satellite TV, inter-active video, computer animation and modern technologies with their inherent power of connecting the entire world have made the process of teaching-learning easy, effective and impressive.

Thus, Educational Technology has revolutionized the entire education system in the world over.

E.T. from the view-point of following sub-systems

(1) Identification and aspirations of the community taking social, cultural, economic and linguistics needs – Audience Profile

(2) Development of learning objectives at primary, elementary, secondary levels – Psycho-social

(3) Development of curriculum – curriculum technology

(4) Organization of learning resources – environmental school, library, museum – learning resource technology

(5) Organization of training programme – T.T. Technology

(6) Development of instructional material (books, guides, A.V. aids – Edl. media technology.)

(7) Development of formative and summative evaluation tools – Evaluation technology

(8) Development of framework and detailed requirements of schools, personnel, space, training, budget and time frame – Edl. Management Technology

EDUCATIONAL MEDIA

Media in education is not educational technology. In a country where one is dealing with enormously large numbers – one-third of the population is illiterate, 60 percent of the children drop out, etc. it becomes important not only to consider improvement in quality of teachers but also the reach of education. Simple direct learning materials are important where student-teacher interaction takes place and broadcasting through radio and television assumes significance as a technology to only in the most difficult conditions.

The Educational Media (EM) can broadly be classified into-

1) Non-machine devices (e.g. charts, maps, globes, cutouts, flashcards, models, toys, puzzles and games).
2) Machine-operated devices (e.g. filmstrips, slides, OHP transparencies, audio and video cassettes films).

Media education are likely to be used only when they fulfill a need, are of superior quality and are accessible to the learner through teachers or directly.

Production of Software

Software production for educational media requires a combination of knowledge of subject, media production techniques and communication strategy to reach the target audience. Merely copying a diagram from a book into a large sheet of paper does not necessarily make a good chart. Nor does just recording a chapter of book gives either a good audio or video tape. The media (print or electronic) are only tools for communication and some basic questions need answering and understanding before production can be usefully undertaken. Among them are:

(1) Communication for whom?
(2) With what needs?
(3) With what objectives?
(4) With what past experiences?
(5) With what means and medium?
(6) By whom?
(7) With what advance preparation?
(8) With what organizational administrative framework?
(9) What targets are feasible in terms of time and money to produce quality materials?

One can appropriately state two classes of media characteristics, viz. essential media characteristics and optional media characteristics.

Essential media characteristics are the ones which control the clarity of the message. For instance, the working of an engine of a motor vehicle demands a moving visual presentation which could be a TV, film or computer-aided device which may even demand a slow motion picture or a film presentation. Learning a language requires print and audio media. This is in the category of essential media.

Optional media characteristics involve the improvement of the quality of presentation. So there are number of considerations on which the selection of a particular type of media is based. We may choose a media which is attractive to the learner or in which he/she is involved in the process of preparation of that aid. The use of media also depends upon the learning tasks, systematic analysis and the objectives of the content. These are listed as under:

Availability, cost effectiveness, feasibility (electricity, material, learner), Quality etc.

Media selection depends up on:

Subject matter and the required learner performance

Types of learning tasks Methods of selection Practical constraints and teacher attitude

Characteristics of learner Media selection

So the main questions for the selection of media are:

1. Can it be obtained/made at an economical price?
2. Is there enough space to use it effectively?
3. Will it work under the relevant conditions (temperature, power, sources, transport-ability, etc.)?
4. Is it learner-proof (not prone to vanish)?
5. Is it capable of being maintained if required?
6. Does it have reasonable life?

Thus, it is very important for us to understand as to how we mediate with the media.

□

3

COMMUNICATION AND ITS PROCESSES

According to the founder Director of the Indian Institute of Mass Communication, Shri L.R. Nair "Communication is the process of transmitting information, ideas and attitudes from one or more persons to others."

Various models for communications have been suggested. These are mainly of two types : psychological models which examine and explain the interaction between the learners and their environment, i.e. who says what, to whom, under what conditions and with what effect. The others are the engineering models which explain the process such as inputs, output and more importantly time, message. These are in the form of field of experience as below:

Sender or Encoder—Signal—Decoder or Receiver

The Elaborated version is

as under :

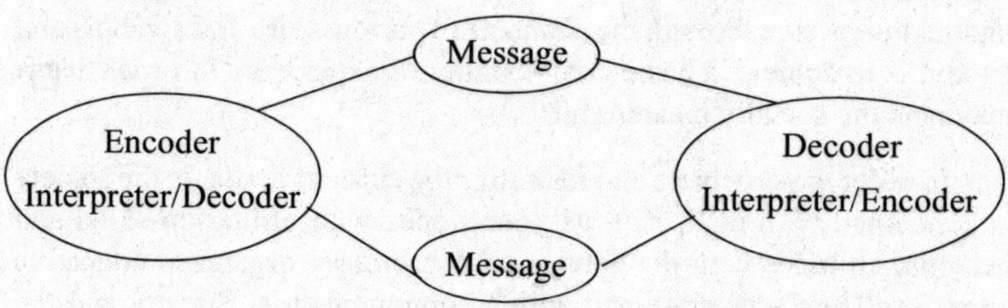

Conditions of Success in Communication

1. Message must gain the attention of the audience.
2. Message must employ signs which refer to experience common to source and destination "get the meaning across".
3. Message must across personality needs in the destination and suggest some ways to meet those needs.
4. Message must suggest a way to meet those needs which are appropriate to the group.

Objectives in Communication

(1) To entertain
(2) To inform
(3) To impart skills
(4) To present concepts or organised knowedge
(5) To correlate knowledge with problems
(6) To provoke thinking, arouse curiosity
(7) To stimulate imagination and creativity
(8) To trigger action towards problem solving
(9) To modify attitudes and behaviour
(10) To bring about change.

What is Audio-Visual Communication

1. Importance of Communication

Education is an active process of socialization, and learning no longer remains as an individualized and centralized mental process. Learning in a social setting has various ramifications and has given birth to a comprehensive term comrnunication. Communication is a process of mutual interaction through the channels of various cues and symbols and its aim is to achieve a basic commonality of experience in order that it may become socially meaningful.

In order to perpetuate and revitalize the cultural heritage, the society is concerned with equipping its young ones with utilitarian skills and personal attitudes with the help of its consciously organized educative agencies. They accelerate and enrich communication. Society and the individual are the only two media of the process of human communication.

The modern educator is most vitally concerned with the phenomena of interpersonal communication. He has set himself to the challenging task of helping students achieve desired social and vocational adjustment through democratic learning experiences, based upon the interests and needs of the children. With the availability and currency of multifarious media of communication, a rich variety of means can be harnessed to achieve desired goals in education. It is important for effective communication to fit the medium to the goals.

2. Defining Communication

Communication is derived from the Latin word communis, meaning common. In the process of communicating an information or a state of mind, a commonness is established between two or more persons.

"Communication is a two way sharing process, not a movement along a one-way track. To communicate is to make an idea common to two or more persons."

The frame of reference of communication is all-embracing when we use it in a very broad sense to include all of the procedures by which one mind may affect another. This, of course, involves not only written and oral speech but also music, the pictorial arts, the theatre, the ballet, and in fact all human behaviour.

To stresse the importance of cues or stimuli we can say that communication is the process by which an individual or group transmits cuse, predominantly verbal to modify the behaviours of another inidividual or group.

The range of communication is from face-to-face to mass. Face-to-face communication involves more "sense modalities" or cues. It also provides immediate "feed-back" or a reconstructing and orientating situation. Mass communication differs from face-to-face to the extent that "(a) The number of modalities is minimized. (b) Orientative feed-back is minimized or delayed."

The communication situation has certain basic elements. It is a dynamic organization of the communicator or sender, interpreter or receiver and communication content or message.

The sender may be an individual (speaking, writing, drawing or gesturing) or a communication organization (like a newspaper, publishing house, television station, or motion picture studio). The message may be in the form of ink on paper, sound waves in the air, impulses in an electric current, a wave of the hand, a flag in the air, or any other signal capable of being interpreted meaningfully. The receiver may be an individual listening, watching, reading; or a member of a group, such as a discussion group, a lecture audience, or a football crowd, or a mob; or a member of the mass audience such as the reader of a news paper or a viewer of television.

The content of communication is an organized field of stimuli consisting of a variety of signs and symbols produced by a communicating agency and perceived through single or multi-sensory channels. The entire domain of communication with its specialized section of audio-visual aids is vitally concerned with sign-symbol materials and media.

3. The Contents of Communication

While communicating, it is impossible to carry about actual objects involved or to go to the places or persons involved. It is laborious to explain the feelings and concepts as well. So we use signs and symbols to represent them. They produce stimuli which create desired reactions in the persons involved.

Mead has recognized the enormous implications for society of the symbol-using processes. For him symbols are not merely sense-stimuli to which mental states-"meanings","concepts", ideas, etc. have become attached. They are the main source of the commonness of the experiences of the persons involved in communication.

A sign is a signal that stands for something else in experience. "But there is an important difference between the sign and the object. The sign always represents the object at a reduced level of cues."

4. The Process of Communication

Coordinating the elements and contents of communication, as analysed above, we weave a complete pattern or process of communication. Wilbur Schramm has a pioneering contribution in this domain when he crystallizes this process.

The sender and encorder are one person, decoder and receiver are another, and this signal is the language or content of communication. When the sender wants to build up a commonness with the receiver, he encodes his message or he puts the information or feeling to be shared in a form that conveys the meaning. All these different forms or media are covered by the media of communication or the audio-visual materials or aids. These materials emit signals or stimuli which are perceived by the receiver. He decodes the message according to his perceptual set, motive, need, values, interests, etc. Experience has a vital role to play in the entire domain of communication. The senders or the receivers project fields of experience. These fields have got to overlap partially, only then the signals can be discerned. We present a modified symbolic form of the process of communication. Mark the dominant role played by the audio-visual materials. It still further clasifies and pinpoints the fact that the audio-visual aids develop information, skills and attitudes. They reduce the over-verbalization in teaching and thus provide a concrete basis for learning.

5. The Cycle of Communication

Professor Erik Barnouw, while explaining the psychology of mass communication outlines distinct stages which constitute the communication cycle- serial steps in which communication progresses.

(i) Expectation

Communication should be nearer to its audience, viewer, reader or listener. At the time of reception of the message, a receiver has a particular perceptual set in which certain expectations, based upon his needs, are prominent. The message is related to his expectations.

(ii) Attention

The contents and media of communication must invite attention. The sender of the message does it by increasing sensationalism in artwork, attractive headlines, sound effects, book covers and various other devices.

(iii) Emotion

When attention is excited, deeper emotions are tapped. A state of aroused emotions brings the receiver nearer the sender.

(iv) Information

After the arousal of emotion, comes the opportune time of giving the information or the message. The earlier stages of the cycle have motivated proper reception.

(vi) Action

Ideas determine actions. In mass communication certain drives are awakened and they demand expression through action.

(v) Idea

Often the content of communication has a dominant idea. This has the greater impact on the receiver for imbibing it into his needs.

6. Audio-Visual Materials

In the entire process of communication the contribution of audio-visual aids or materials stands out prominently. They constitute the only and exclusive media or channels of communication. We term them popularly, as audio-visual, since about 85 to 90 percent of the signals or sense-stimuli enter our perception through the eyes and the ears. A broad background of perceptual experience is the basis for learning and communication. Our perceptor sensory mechanisms "the eyes, the ear, the nerve endings which respond to pressure, to heat and cold, and to odours and tastes" are constantly in contact with our environment. Since all the senses provide stimuli for our perceptual reorganization and integration, so sometime these materials which make us learn are termed as multi-sensory materials.

The audio-visual method of learning is as old as humanity itself, but in the professional literature there are many technical terms of recent origin which are intimately and closely allied to audio-visual materials "visual education", "visual instruction", "visual aids", "audio visual instruction", "audio-visual aids!", "audio-visual, training aids", "multi-sensory aids", "visual-sensory aids", etc.

Edgar Dale presents an absolutely new approach when he remarks- "Although we commonly use the term audio-visual, it is merely a shorthand way of describing materials of instruction which are less abstract than words themselves. Even here we must exercise care because it would be more accurate to call them audio-visual-verbal materials because these relatively more concrete experiences are nearly always skilfully integrated with words themselves."

7. Audio-visual communication is that phenomenon or process whereby identical messages are conveyed to different persons through the agency of audio-visual materials or mass media as instruments of communication. Analysing the fundamental mental processes involved, in learning and communication, we find that we can trace many identical and overlapping concepts in the theoretical analysis of both these terms. Learning, communication, education, instruction, teaching are often used as synonymous terms.

Technicians, psychologists, linguists, sociologists and whole lot of professionals in one way or the other are concerned with the development of communication, its nature and functions. The concept of communication is a seminal problem. Its domain is an ever widening, embracing the entire range of human lives and activities. In education the methodology has gone far ahead but in the field of communication theory and research it is lagging behind the media which are moving on with rapid speed.

Perception with a background of human experience available in the form of symbolic formulation is the nucleus of the theoretical work in communication. Dale has explained the importance of multi sensory experiences integrated through perception and focused at the gap between the known information on the perception. The major problem of the communication theories is not a paucity of the hypothesis but lack of comprehending the structures.

Contents of Communication

While communicating, it is possible to carry about actual objects involved or to go to the places. It is important to explain the feelings and concepts also. There are situations in learning and communication. Infact, the permanence of learning is the result of effective communication. So the psychology of learning is a major component of the theory of communication. Any concept of communication is bound to be phenomenal. It has to take into account all the cues in the environment to study any one of the related parts of the organism whole of experience. The concept of perception and the psychology of learning help us to penetrate deeper as we highlight different parts of the entire field in the light of totality of thought.

Visual Communication

Visuals communicate a lot more information than the words. While selecting visiuals one has to be very careful so that only intended communication takes place. Following points may be taken while selecting visuals for communication :

(a) A visual may communicate unintended message. While selecting visual, examine them from this viewpoint also.

(b) Audio/video pointers may have to be used for a particular visual to focus the attention of the viewer.

(c) Efforts should be made to communicate one message with one visual. Too many messages with one visual may be confusing for the viewer.

(d) While using a complex graphic/visual either start from the whole show the parts or build up the visual/graphic from parts to the whole.

(e) Some visuals may need audio support to reinforce/clarity/or even add on to the message Audio should not be used to describe the visuals.

□

4

TECHNOLOGICAL AIDS

Audio-visual aids have been in use in the Indian Education System since ancient times. These aids are also known as teaching aids as these are helpful to the teachers and to the learners. The emphasis from teaching has been changing fast and it is the learning which is most significant. The teachers teach so that the learners could learn which is the ultimate objective of teaching-learning.

With the passages of time the teaching-learning process is more effective with the help of materials as the books alone do not help to comprehend the concepts. Books are static and the concepts involving mobility are difficult to understand without the help of teaching aids. Concepts in science involving motion such as the working of engine, the functions of inner parts can best be explained with the help of working models or through animation, computer-aided instructions or motion pictures. But it is not necessary that we have to make use of teaching aids for all the concepts. If a concept can be explained or demonstrated by taking the students outside in the immediate, environment, there is hardly any use of preparing a chart or a poster to explain the concept. What is required is the scientific outlook and to critically observe the nature and the immediate environment of the learner which is rich to discover the world around the children.

The process of teaching-learning material is also undergoing a dynamic change with the advent of new innovations of science and technology. It is perhaps more relevant to give a new nomenclature to the teaching aids as teaching-learning resources which is more comprehensive.

Teaching-learning materials are lifeless and we are employing these lifeless tools for human beings, the learners and the teachers who form a significant part of life. Thus, it is more relevant to talk of teaching-learning resources rather than teaching-learning materials.

Before understanding a thing the children-need scientific experience of seeing, touching, hearing, tasting and smelling and experimenting with the real things of life which they always do while going to school from their homes. They observe nature and communicate among themselves to get various experiences. But they need help to get the material. When they achieve something successfully, they get the joy and happiness and also gain confidence which encourages them to learn and to attempt further activities. Young children learn best from simple things and it is most helpful to them to understand those things first that are around them in their daily lives.

Unicef Source Book "Preparation for Understanding" by Keith Warren elaborates this idea of discovery.

Low cost Technological Aids in Indian Education – An Experiment

The programe of Low Cost technological Aids was initiated and carried out with a credo and philosophy of an ancient poet who said:

"Go in search of your people, love them, learn from them, plan with them, begin with what they know, build on what they have".

Low cost teaching aids are made out material from the natural environment, waste and craft products; they are low cost items available in the neighbourhood and are made by teachers, children or artisans, using local craft and technology rather than machines. The aids are distinctly different from radio, television, slides, film projectors and other such devices, which in certain applications may also be cost-effective and 'low cost' but for the purpose a distinction will be drawn between the two. It may seem paradoxical to talk of low cost appropriate material for educational aids in an era of satellite communication and computer-aided instruction. Yet, in a country where 80 per cent of the people live in villages, where schools do not have enough funds to buy equipment, low cost aids are essential, if the ultimate objective of a developing society is to live in harmony with nature and not to conquer it.

The developing countries have frequently imported hardware to modernize their education systems. They have also imported software which may not have been suited to the needs of their own language and culture. Unlike the West, where the development of educational hardware and software took place side by side over the years, some developing countries like India, have made technological progress in the development of hardware but the culture of educational media and in particular the software has not grown significantly. Although India has a rich tradition of art, craft and magic emanating from the imagination and skills of the rural people, formal education in rural India makes little use of it. Instead the education system is based on syllabi and an examination system designed and administered in the urban capitals of the State which have a different ethos and culture. Sixty per cent of children drop out at the primary level since the school education is not geared towards their lives and goals. Those who get through the system often find themselves misfit. in the villages and drift to the cities to join the ever-growing multitudes of the unemployed. Thus, the rural school does not foster the cultural and economic development of the community.

So where does one begin? How does one relate education to the environment and rich cultural heritage? How does one do it cheaply without making it a burden on the educational system or uprooting it? And above all, how can the culture of educational media and software grow at the grassroots level in villages and small towns? It is not easy to begin to answer these questions as they are so inter-linked.

An Experiment

A series of workshops were organized in different parts of the country by the Department of Teaching Aids, National Council of Educational Research and Training, New Delhi from 1976 onwards to look for some of the answers. The basic objectives of the programme were:

1. To interact and communicate with rural and tribal primary teachers in understanding their problems in education and school.
2. To help the rural teachers create and develop teaching aids relevant to their own environment which could be made within the meagre annual budget of the school (per year).
3. To use community resources, such as artisans and craftsmen and local materials, for the development of teaching aids.
4. To involve the state level agencies (education in India is predominantly governed by each state) in the workshops and draw upon their experiences.

5. To understand how such micro-level attempts could diffuse to the macro-level.

Two-way Communication

It is customary to believe that workshops bring together experts from the city and teachers from villages and that there is essentially a one-way flow of communication from the 'know-all' experts to the 'ignorant' teachers. We also began the workshops with this view, giving lectures on different types of aids, showing various examples of two-and three-dimensional aids, and how to draw simply. This approach would have continued but for the keen perceptions and criticism of the rural workers at the first workshop. They argued that such a method would not encourage any initiative from the teachers and artisans. It would mean enforcing our 'urban' thinking on them. Instead shouldn't we raise questions with them and build some two-way communication? It was immediately recognized the wisdom in this and revision of approach.

After discussion in which the teachers talked about the problems they faced in the classroom, we showed the teachers and artisans were exposed to several puzzles and some models of mechanical water pumps. Their reaction was fascinating. Some of the artisans not only solved the puzzles but also came up with some suggestions for improving the water pumps. The teachers were more passive. As most of them belonged to the higher caste they were not used to working with their own hands and were initially reluctant to do so. On the other hand, some of them were enthusiastic when asked to make an aid. They selected some diagrams from their science books and began with great zeal to prepare charts. From them, copying them word by word and adding decorative borders to the colorful presentation. Only a few teachers prepared any models.

In subsequent work shops we asked selected teachers to bring a specimen of the aids used by them. Only a few responded; others had no aids or brought charts which had been prepared specifically for the workshop. In any case, these aids brought by the teachers, whatever their worth, helped to break the ice in the programme.

During analysis and discussion, some of the questions were more coherently raised by the rural workers and teachers themselves. For example, why use an aid? Something which can be clearly taught through a book, a blackboard and the words of the teacher do not require an aid. If however, it is not clear through ordinary classroom teaching then what can a teacher do? These questions arose from thinking about a chart on the growth of peanuts. None of the teachers saw the error in it even though peanuts were grown in the area; it was pointed out by the rural worker. Since peanuts were grown in the area, whether it would not be better to take the children to a farm in the neighbourhood? Is a chart the best medium for such a topic? If so, what is the crucial information it can give which the textbook cannot? How should it be presented? Who will make the chart and how can it be used?

The Products

After identifying the difficulties in teaching at the primary level and discussing the logic of using aid, there came the point of making an aid. Some of the materials had also been identified. For each workshop (about four to five days) the teachers, artisans and resource persons would design and develop the aids in different groups. By the third and fourth workshop a format was evolved. The teachers would prepare a brief project document covering the objectives of the aid; the material required; the method of preparation (with as many drawings) as possible showing the different stages; the applications and the approximate cost. After procuring the material they began work on its production. The rough preparation was then analyzed and discussed in groups in a general session. Some of the enthusiastic teachers undertook more than one project. Some modified the crude one, developed by them on the basis of the comment received.

On the last day of the workshop an educationist or a scientist visited the workshop to see and comment on the aids produced by the teachers. On a few occasions children were invited to come and see the exhibition.

The products prepared in these workshops were crude. There was a consideration if it would be possible to refine them. Should it be done in Delhi? If so, the materials would not have rural characteristics. They might turn into slick models and this could dissuade the teachers from attempting to make them themselves. Therefore, it was necessary to refine them at the rural level. How could we do that in ten days? It was felt that with new teachers we had to spend half the time explaining the philosophy and building rapport with them. We therefore decided to ask four of the better teachers from each of our earlier workshops to attend the fifth, so that the new participants would learn from their experiences. The fifth workshop, therefore, was essentially to refine the material produced earlier in a form which would be neat but not too sophisticated. We did not want the teachers in this workshop to look for difficult and new concepts but rather to work on the concepts and materials developed earlier and to explore ways in which the idea could best be put into practice. For example, there were four problems with the Newton's disc of seven spectral colours; how much area should be given to each of the colours on the disc; what shade and intensity should the colours be; what kind of material would best hold the painted colours; and how could the disc be rotated fast enough to produce the near white effect? The teachers studied and explored various materials, colours and methods of rotation. They tried mounting a piece of painted card around the axle of the rear wheel of a bicycle which could be rotated on its stand. They took an empty tin of boot polish and tried rotating it with the help of threads going through two holes. This came close to producing the desired effect. The process required questioning, some research, the making and testing of practical models and raised the idea of further improvement. The corollary, that of breaking the white light into seven colours, was similarly explored by making a water prism out of slides and joining them by wax.

A Wider Dissemination

Several questions emerged that were similar to those at the previous ones. How could the teachers build on this experience? How could they be informed in their remote village about new ideas? How could the making of aids become a continuous and dynamic process? Would the administration recognize these efforts, etc.? To start with workshops at the rural level (with local teachers, artisans and state resource persons), would generate the methodology as well as the aids. These could be refined and then a manual produced with diagrams showing how aids could be prepared locally and cheaply. The manual could be on open sale as well as available through state education authorities. The teachers should not only receive the book but be encouraged to make aids both those in the manual and others. In the second part of the cycle, the aids prepared by the teachers could be exhibited at block and district level and receive recognition by the state authorities. The ideas could be selected by a national body for wider distribution through publication and the rural workshops. These rural workshops would not only be organized by the national or central organization but would multiply through state institutes or organizations generating more ideas and more action. These two parts would constitute the dynamic process through which teachers would be involved at the grass roots level and where diffusion from micro-level could hopefully take place.

Conclusion

The example mentioned above is only one amongst several in the country. Some draw more into their programme than others but all face the difficulties as well as the challenges arising out of the explosion of population and knowledge and a shortage of resources. The syllabus is heavily loaded and the small number of teachers are not adequately trained to handle it. The major emphasis is, therefore, not on learning but on teaching so that pupils do well in the examinations. Under such circumstances, the efforts described above are just a drop in the ocean. But! think they are worth pursuing.

Why Teaching Aids?

Their significance and Use in the teaching-learning Process

'Teaching Aids' is a term which is inadequately understood. It means different things to different persons. To some it means television, films, or charts and posters. Others think they are slides, pictures, maps clay models, etc., till others associate the term with the skills of drawing and model-making. All these skills and media are in fact used for preparing teaching aids, but the terms do relate to any one of them.

That different meaning are attached to the term 'teaching aids' is quite natural. In our country, diverse socio-economic conditions prevail. Teachers in different parts of the country are not uniformly exposed to the various media. A teacher in a city may have seen television and films but to their counterparts in the villages these sophisticated media are new and unfamiliar.

The teacher may be familiar with the different teaching aids, but it is one thing to be familiar with them and quite another to know the use to which they can be put or to have skill to prepare a teaching aid.

The objective is to discuss some teaching aids which the teacher may be able to prepare from materials available in the rural environment. For many years to come television, films and slides would be difficult to obtain and use at the rural level. It is, therefore, necessary to focus attention on the teaching aids which can be produced with village resources and used at the rural level.

Production of effective teaching aids is not a simple task. Teaching aids would be effective and meaningful only when the producer of such aids is aware of the following:

(a) The value of good teaching;
(b) Knowledge of the subject matter;
(c) The learning potential of the learners;
(d) The basic principles of the content and the process of learning;
(e) The relationship of the content with the environment;
(f) Local resources, including human resources; and
(g) Interest in the subject and the learners.

Besides the above point, there are several other aspects which need to be understood in the context of teaching aids. In most schools nearly all the subjects and principles related to them are taught with the emphasis on learning by rote. Before preparing teaching aids it is necessary to understand precisely what it is that the learners do not understand through the book or verbally. Why not take them out of the classroom to make certain concepts clear? There would be no point in making chart of a peanut plant or a mango tree, when by merely stepping out of the classroom one could show them to the children and tell them the functions of the parts of plants seeds, roots, fruits, etc.

Similarly, many concepts could be explained through simple experiments with objects available in the environment or brought from the house. The concept of "pressure of air" can be demonstrated with an experiment that just requires a glass, water and a piece of cardboard. Making a chart would be meaningful only when some other aspects of pressure are to be explained which cannot be demonstrated in such a simple way. Working with one's own hands or performing an experiment on one's own is invaluable in the learning process. A Chinese proverb states this point very effectively:

When I read, I forgot,
When I see, I understand,
But when I do it myself,
I understand.

Hence, there cannot be a better way to educate children than to have them do experiments meant for their level. To read out a play in the classroom is one thing, but it is more effective to show them the play or have some of them act out. It leaves an indelible impression on their minds. So with experiments it is indeed difficult for schools to organize experiments which children at the primary level could do themselves. One wonders if this is being done anywhere in the country. In the absence of this, what could be done is to demonstrate or show them simple experiments.

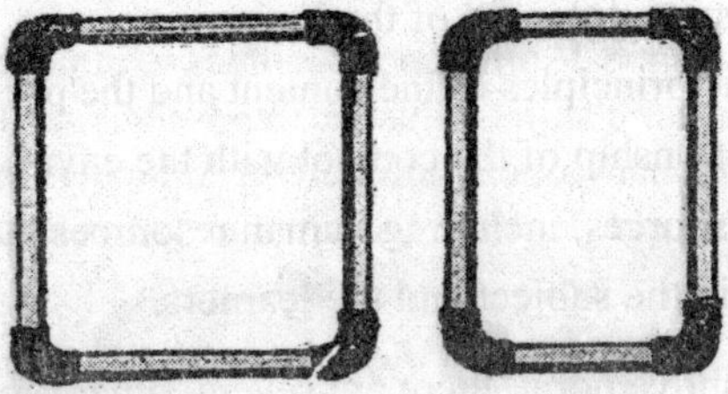

To do all this requires extra efforts by the teacher. To collect different materials and to get models made by local craftsmen may require the development of certain capabilities on the part of the teacher.

The environment is itself a big laboratory. By taking the children out on excursions, tours and walks, a lot of information can be imparted. This concept is relatively new and its potential has not yet been fully realized. For example, if there is a river nearby, then by going there, showing the children the life around, collecting samples, posing questions and making drawings, a lot of information can be imparted and quick learning can take place. On the other hand, by verbal explanation, or simply by drawing a picture, the learning imparted may not be fully absorbed. Other subjects for-on-the-spot study are suggested: water resources, the technology for their use; road traffic and kinds of transportation; the various crafts of the village, products and their uses. Not only can many subjects be taught through such examples but the relationship between a subject and the environment can also be established. Children are fascinated by the environment. It is only a question of planning of studies so that the two are correlated but to do this the teacher would have to work out his her own method.

As is well known, teaching aids include books, the blackboard, experiments and excursions. Then there are aids such as charts, models three-dimensional pictures and games which can make the concept fascinating and learning easy. Many such aids could be designed for learners at various stages. Now let us examine the importance of teaching aids and their relationship with education. Teaching aids should relate to the subject and the teaching method. However, very often, while making teaching aids, we tend to lose sight of our goals. In over-emphasizing the technical perfection and finish of an aid, we often forget the difficulties of the subject or concept and sometimes also the complexities of the teaching-learning process. The colours to be used for the model become more important for the teacher than the content and method of teaching.

Skill and visual appeal sometimes becomes so important that teachers who do not have artistic skills consider themselves inadequate to make teaching aids. There has to be a rationale or logic behind the process of making any teaching aid. It could be stated as follows:

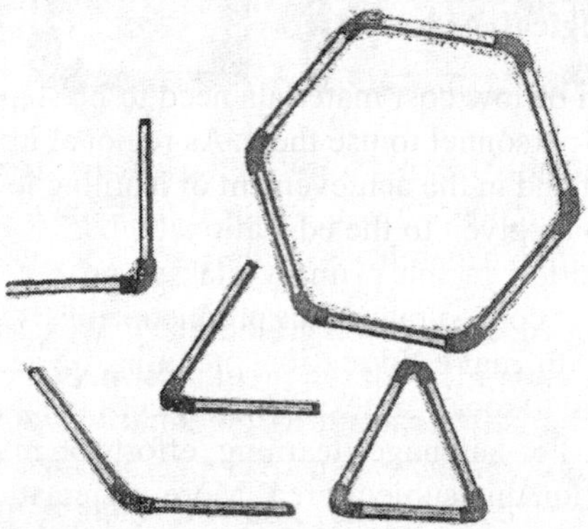

(a) The textbook is not the head and fount of all learning; other sources are as important.
(b) The understanding of the mental level of the learners;
(c) The best way to teach the concept and the various steps involved in it. How should they be sequenced?
(d) The various ways of imparting information in the classroom and outside: verbal, experimental, etc.

When the teacher reaches the conclusion that none of the conventional methods will suffice, only then should he think of preparing an aid. The need of the teaching aid has to be established. Once the rationale becomes clear to the teacher, he may attempt to make one and use it effectively.

The next question is about the type of teaching aid which may be necessary to clarify the concept. Should it be a chart, a model, a picture, a map or a game? After the appropriate medium has been chosen, the question of art or skill comes. Drawing and colouring a chart or making a working model, demands artistic skill. It has its place in the making of teaching aids but it is not a necessary condition. It would also be misleading to think that:

(a) Knowing artistics skills alone suffice in making and using a teaching aid and

(b) If the teacher does not know these skills, which most teachers do not, teaching aids cannot be made.

The objective of preparing and using a teaching aid is to improve the teaching-learning process. To fulfill that need, it is essential to understand the basic concepts of teaching and methodology of teaching.

Low cost Technological Aids

The production of low cost materials need to be stepped up along-with the training of personnel to use them. As regional imbalance exists in school enrolment and in the achievement of learning level of children more attention is to be given to the educationally backward areas. High wastage and stagnation in the primary classes pose problems. It is, therefore, necessary to concentrate on the production of low cost education materials in order to make education meaningful and joyful. The educational potential of local games and toys needs to be explored to be used in the schools. For languages learning, efforts be made to produce low cost materials for this subject area. More systematic work is also needed in producing low cost educational materials for social sciences.

Objectives of preparation and Use of Low cost Education Materials

The objectives for the preparation and use of low-cost educational materials in the schools are:

(i) Create an awareness about the availability of low-cost/no cost material for the preparation of teaching aids.

(ii) Consider the use of locally available resources and other appropriate material for design and development of educational material.

(iii) Develop sample of low-cost simple material together with the instructional sheets for use in instruction.

(iv) Involve the local community-artisans such as carpenters, potters, with the teachers and children to prepare the teaching aids.

(v) Exchange experience in the development of educational materials through display and demonstrations with special emphasis on print, games, toys and other low-cost models and materials.

The current aspirations for improved educational opportunities in India justify greater efforts in the development of low-cost educational materials. The abundance of indigenous raw materials and other resources freely available in the immediate environment which can be utilized into useful educational materials and the rich cultural heritage and traditions which create relevant curricular programs and activities for children, must also be taken into account. The trend to more personal and human teaching-learning especially in developing areas, demands the use of locally available and produced educational materials. Teachers administrators, parents and other members of the community are increasingly aware of and enthusiastic about locally produced educational material to strike a balance with these unattainable, sophisticated and expensive ones.

The need for the low-cost educational materials for the purpose of enhancing the quality of teaching and learning situations has resulted in the initiation of growing activities for developing and using such materials. There is a greater consciousness about the preparation and use of low cost aids. There are similarities as well as differences in the status of such activities.

The contents of the training courses may be categorized as follows:

(i) Need for low-cost educational materials having multiplier effects in the development of education.

(ii) Existing practices in the use of low-cost materials.

(iii) Basic equipment and tools for the design and development of low cost aids.

(iv) Guidelines for developing, using and evaluating the low-cost materials.

(v) Development of prototypes with the instructional sheets.

National Council of Educational Research and Training, New Delhi, State Councils of Educational Research and Training in the States, Distt. Institutes of Education and Training and Teacher Training Institutions/ colleges are vitally concerned with the identification of material at the local level, preparation and use of low-cost materials with appropriate methods The project is being disseminated in the form of a movement in the entire country.

Educational Significance of Low-cost Educational Materials and their need

The educational significance of low-cost educational supporting materials and use of the environment and local resources is increasingly recognized in the Indian school system. The materials, being economical, not only help to cope with the problem of lack of resources for meeting the increasing educational needs implied in national development plans but also, being related to the situations of the learners, strengthen the learning process to a great extent. It is an established fact now that effective learning depends largely upon the learner's motivation for learning as well as upon instruction being made meaningful and purposeful. This can be accomplished to a large extent by using teaching aids, improvised by low-cost indigenous materials through active participation of the learners themselves.

Advantage of Low-Cost Educational Aids

In India, there hardly exists good opportunity for the procurement of expensive and sophisticated educational equipment for all educational institutions incurring heavy expenditure. Even if it becomes possible, the learners, specially in the lower grades, could hardly conceptualize the working principles of the equipment and develop meaningful concepts by using it. On the other hand, low-cost educational aids motivate the child's learning by arousing his interest in a number of ways.

(i) The aids are prepared from inexpensive materials available in the immediate environment of the learners. The novelty of the developing process of the aids makes them attractive and meaningful to the students following the principle of "learning by Doing".

(ii) A pleasant and natural atmosphere is created in the classrooms where aids are improvised through active participation of both the teachers and the taught. It contributes greatly to learning.

(iii) Low-cost educational materials, being simple, are easily understood by the learners. They offer good opportunities to do something and hence provide an added appeal to the learners. As the teachers, along with their students, plan and produce their own educational materials, they are in a position to utilize them. Pupils' participation in the preparation of educational materials stimulates learning and develops skills. Low-cost material can indeed go a long way to provide learners with meaningful learning situations and with ample food for inquiring minds. Because of their simplicity, they easily appeal to pupils in general. They can handle such materials themselves and try them out even in their homes."

WHY LOW-COST MATERIALS ARE REQUIRED

Needs for low-cost educational materials for good quality education are greatly, emphasized. Such needs are in connection with the following:

(i) Inadequacy of necessary financial support for education;

(ii) High rate of population growth, and resulting in increasing number of children in the school-age group;

(iii) Under-use of rich environmental resources in the educational process;

(iv) Provision of adequate educational materials with limited budgetary allocation for education for the schools of under-developed and sometime multi-racial regions in order to overcome disparities in educational opportunities; and

(v) Enhancement of the educational process and improvement of quality teaching in the classroom, because low-cost materials:

   (a) Make learning activities more relevant to environmental context of the learners;

   (b) Make the subject comprehensible and arouse pupils' interest and attention;

   (c) Are easy to handle and more convenient to use by the teachers and pupils;

   (d) Stimulate and motivate the children's interest because of novelty and the element of curiosity and interest in them;

   (e) Avoid the dehumanizing effect of the complicated technology in the form of sophisticated teaching aids.

From what has been synthesized in connection with the needs of low-cost educational materials, it can broadly be said that improving educational standards, expansion of educational opportunities, reduction of environmental wastage and scarcity of financial resources are some of the major constraints in the development of education. In order to overcome these constraints the authorities are taking an increasing interest in low-cost technology as one of the means of improving education in accordance with national development goals.

Low-Cost Materials in INDIA

Low-cost educational materials in India are being produced at the national, state and school levels. The universalization of elementary and adult education are the two priority programmes in India today, and low-cost educational materials are required for both. Their production is to be stepped up, as is the training of personnel to use them. As regional imbalances exist in school enrolment and in the achievement level of children, more attention is to be given to the educationally backward states.

High wastage and stagnations in the early primary classes also pose problems in India. It is therefore necessary to concentrate on the production of low-cost educational materials for young children.

Teacher training needs special attention. Production of low-cost educational materials will be effective only if teachers have sufficient knowledge and under-standing of child development. Pre-service and in-service training of teachers should focus on the child, through the optimum use of educational technology. Recent research studies have shown that home variables playa very important role in the educational achievement of children in India. Keeping this in view, it is necessary to give some attention to the production of educational materials for parents too.

To achieve quality education, the orientation of key personnel on the values of low-cost educational materials is necessary. The powerful media such as television, radio, films and even programmed learning get the major share of attention and budget, whereas low-cost media such as play materials and games tend to be overlooked.

1. Step up efforts to produce low-cost educational materials for the educationally backward states.
2. Survey traditional play materials and games for children teachers, manuals spelling out their education.
3. Produce similarly illustrated materials for the children.
4. Strengthen science education by producing its for teachers in the development and understanding of materials for science education.

5. Begin devising and producing sufficient low-cost aids in the social sciences.
6. Conduct more in-service training programmes for educators in devising and using low-cost educational materials.
7. Develop suitable materials for orienting parents in the educational materials for child development and include pamphlets, slides and posters.
8. Create a lobby for such low-cost educational materials so that they get their rightful place in education.
9. Encourage professional associations involved in the .... Pre-school education to promote the production and use of low-cost aids.
10. Organize contests for teachers in producing low-cost aids.
11. Encourage the setting up of display centres of low-cost materials at State levels.
12. Low-cost aids to be an integral part of Sarva Shiksha Abhiyan with adequate provision of funds.

Low Cost Technological Aids-Characteristics

- The raw materials are freely and easily available from local environment
- The materials can be made by teachers and pupils
- The materials can be put into effective use by the teachers and pupils in the classroom
- The production process of the materials should be easy and less time consuming.

Importance of Technological Aids

- To bring variety in teaching-learning process
- To promote active involvement of learner in learning process
- It has the potential to create conducive self -learning situations for children "teach yourself"
- It helps learner not only to learn, but also recall more and with greater ease at later stage.

Objectives of Workshop

- To enhance the quality of elementary education by using different types of low cost teaching aids in teaching-learning process

- To enable the master trainers/teachers to know about different types of low cost teaching aids in Langauges, Maths, EVS and Science
- To Identify difficult concepts in various subject areas at the Elementary Level
- To enable them to identify locally available material for preparation of different types of low cost teaching aids relevant to their own environment.

Expected Outcomes

- The teacher trainer will be able to provide in-service training on preparation and use of low-cost technological aids in teaching-learning process
- To enable the teachers to prepare and use different types of teaching aids for effective transaction learning experiences
- It is also expected that such teaching aids can be developed and used by the students to construct knowledge and enhance their learning.

Problems of Effective Utilization

- Lack of awareness
- Inadequate skills
- Lack of time
- Inadequate facilities
- Low level of incentives.

Strategies to Overcome the Problems

- More in-service and pre-service training of teachers on the development of low-cost technological aids
- Reducing teaching load and extra work
- Providing manuals of competencies and guides on production and utilization
- Provide appropriate incentives

Low Cost Teaching Aids – Why?

1. Inadequate funds

2. Kits have –
   Problems of maintenance
   Training of teachers
   Lack student-teacher involvement
   Not environmental based
3. Provides scientific base
4. Enables to appreciate other aids
5. Teaching learning more fascinating.

*Chalkboards is the only teaching aid available to the teachers

*Schools suffer heavily for want of funds-no sufficient funds to buy teaching aids

*Teaching aids procured from the market hardly used by teachers due to the latent fear of misplacement/breakage and accountability factor

*Abundance of material available in the immediate environment for fabrication of aids by involving local community, teachers and the children

*Preparation and use of teaching aids bring confidence and helps save money

Schools in dilapidated buildings with storage problems

The contents of the training courses are more or less the same, which may be categorized the contents as follows:

(i) Need for low-cost educational materials having multiplier effects in the development of education;

(ii) Existing practices in the use of low-cost materials;

(iii) Basic tools necessary for designing and developing aids and indigenous raw materials (unused and under-used) that could be used in the preparation of the aids;

(iv) Guidelines for developing, using and evaluating the low-cost materials; and

(v) Actual development of prototypes with instruction sheets.

Significant progress has already been made in designing and developing low-cost educational materials from indigenous sources. The usual practice to design and develop a material is the following:

(i) Setting the objective with respect to curriculum (who needs the aids, what kind, what topic to be covered, etc.).

(ii) Examing the clarity, impact, simplicity, appropriateness and cost of the aid;

(iii) Design and development of the prototypes;

(iv) Trying it out and modifying where needed.

NCERT/SCERTS are concerned with design and development of prototypes with emphasis on low-cost materials for science, mathematics and vocational subjects.

Review of activities on Low-cost Educational Materials

The need for the low-cost educational materials for the purpose of enhancing the quality of teaching and learning situations resulted in the initiation of growing activities for developing and using such materials. There are similarities as well as certain differences in the status of such activities.

Objectives

(i) Preparation of a national inventory of low-cost educational materials including educational games and toys;

(ii) Development of new prototypes of low-cost materials with corresponding instruction sheets;

(iii) Setting up of national guidelines for the design, development, distribution, use and evaluation of the materials;

(iv) Identification of unused, and under-used materials and basic tools for production of low-cost materials; and

(v) Training of teachers and concerned personnel to intensity awareness of the values and needs for using low-cost educational materials for improving the quality of education and overcome limited financial allocation to schools, and to learn innovative techniques and methods for preparation of such materials as envisaged in the national guidelines.

The Present status of the Development of Low-cost Educational Materials

The current aspirations for improved educational opportunities in India justify greater efforts in the development of low-cost educational materials. The abundance of indigenous raw materials and other resources which can be utilized into useful educational materials, and the rich cultural heritages and traditions from which to create relevant curriculum programmes and activities for children, must also be taken into account. The trend to more personal and human teaching, especially in developing areas, demands the optimum use of locally-produced educational materials. Teachers, administrators, parents and other concerned people in the community are increasingly aware of and enthusiastic about locally produced educational materials. All of these factors encourage the development of low-cost educational materials to balance those unattainable, sophisticated and expensive ones.

Problems and Issues Related to Iow-Cost Educational Materials

A. Personnel

Lack of skilled and trained teachers and supervisors. In some cases, the teachers do not use the available educational materials. They are not part of preparation process.

B. Materials

Insufficient quantity of manpower and lack of the tools needed to prepare educational materials. The schools in the distant localities are most affected by this problem.

C. Distribution

Poor transportation facilities for the delivery of educational materials, supplies and equipment.

D. Use of Materials

In distant localities, teachers have very limited knowledge about the importance and use of low-cost educational materials. This accounts for the unused materials found in store-rooms or cupboards in many schools.

Annotated List of Low-Cost Educational Materials Developed

1. Right-angled triangle to construct various geometrical shapes a simple square paper which can be folded into as many geometrical shapes as possible.

2. Prism a very low cost prism made of three glass strips held together by a triangular piece of metal, or plastic sheets and scotch tape.

3. Discarded bulb lens—an inexpensive lens made from a discarded electric light bulb which can be used as a microscope or an optical lens.
4. Spring balance—very simple weighing device made of a flat piece of wood, elastic thread and a metal pointer.
5. Gears different sizes of wooden gears constructed to show the relative revolutions and direction of movement of the gears.
6. Spirit level an ampoule filled with distilled water attached in the centre of a wooden block which can be used to test the uniform level of horizontal surfaces.
7. Map printing can a very simple map printing device made of an empty long cylindrical can and a map which is outlined with thick cotton thread. The cotton thread outline is soaked with ink to print the map as the can is rolled on paper.

Synthesis of the Experiences

The reports from the participants of Low Cost Workshops revealed some problems in actively promoting the development of technology. The contents can be conveniently discussed under the following:

The child and educational materials

Problems in design, development, utilization and evaluation.

National constraints affecting educational technology.

Attitudes and values of teachers, the community, parents and involvement in the development of low-cost educational materials.

The management of educational materials.

Mechanisms for the dissemination low-cost educational materials.

The role of the educational administration and other agencies, promotion of educational materials.

Guidelines on Development of Low-cost Educational Materials

The following measures are suggested to deal with the major problem areas.

(a) To develop creative thinking and inculcate a problem-solving attitude, experimentation on effective ways of organizing and managing the class-room as well as the lesson should be encouraged. For example, in open school system, non-graded classes, team teaching and other innovative approaches can be tried with the optimum use of educational materials, games and toys.

(b) In the schools there are different types of person-to-person interactions such as teacher-to-pupil, pupil-to-pupil and teacher-to-headmaster. Such interactive systems should be so channeled that the atmosphere in the school be conducive to the self-directed development of the child.

(c) Active research on making learning more enjoyable should be carried out and techniques for actively stimulating and sustaining interest explored. Centres such as a child media centre could 'be established specifically for the purpose of focusing on learning that takes place outside the school.

(d) Measures should be taken to influence and inform parents through pamphlets, books and films, about basic aspects of child development, so that the parent-child relationship be improved and help the active development of the child.

(e) There must be a special emphasis on games and plays as part of instructional strategy for fostering child development.

2. Design, Development, Utilization and Evaluation

The bulk of educational materials developed are on science and mathematics, while the social sciences and languages are often overlooked. Accordingly, the following suggestions are made:

(a) Elementary school teaching-learning activities should be so arranged that communication skills are also developed, using educational materials to the fullest.

(b) Workshops should be conducted to develop kits or packages for social sciences and communication arts. These kits might include puppets, toys, study prints, tape recording of speeches, slides and brochures.

The level of research in educational materials in many participating countries is still not of a high quality. For this, the following activities were suggested:

(a) As far as possible researchers in educational technology should incorporate elements of experimental design of low-cost educational materials in their work.

(b) There should be more intensive, systematic evaluation while developing new materials or new strategies for teaching or organizing a lesson. In particular, the effect of the materials and strategies in maintaining curiosity and interest should be assessed.

SOME EXAMPLES

A. Water condenser

Description

This is a simple water condenser which can be used as a substitute for Liebig's water condenser. Unlike the glass condenser, this one does not break when handled because it is made of plastic pipe and plastic tubings.

Objective

To show to students of lower secondary level a simple process of distillation.

Materials Needed

One transparent polythene pipe, 9" long (23 cm) and 1" (2.5 cm) in diameter.

One piece of transparent polythene tubing, two yards (or 2 meters) long.

Two short pieces of transparent polythene tubing.

Two rubber stoppers for the pipe with two holes each through which the piece of tubing will fit.

How to Make

Insert the long polythene tubing into one of the holes in the stopper.

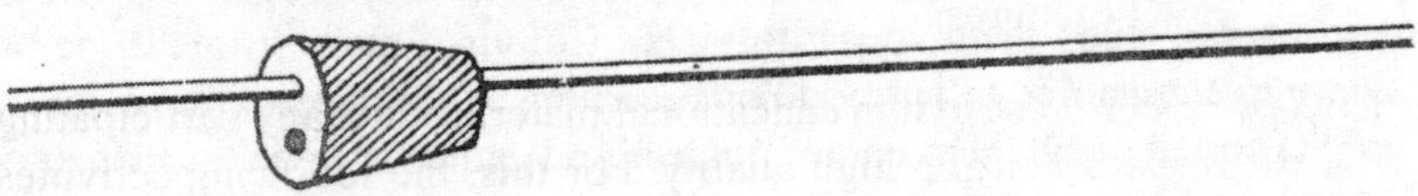

Fix the stopper into one end of the pipe.

Insert the end of the tubing that comes out of the pipe into one of the holes of the other stopper and fix this stopper into the pipe.

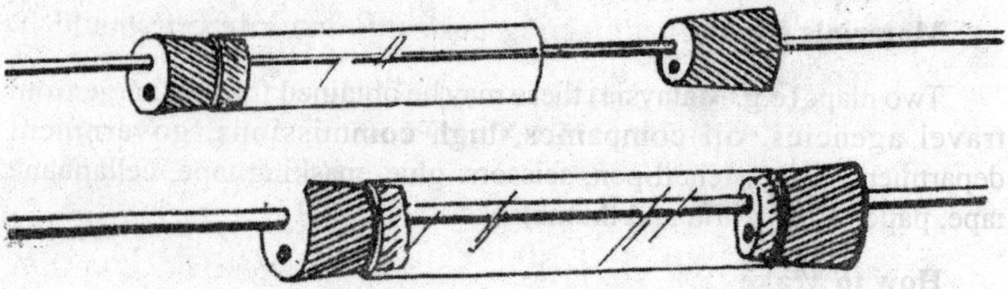

Insert the two short pieces of polythene tubing into the remaining holes of each stopper.

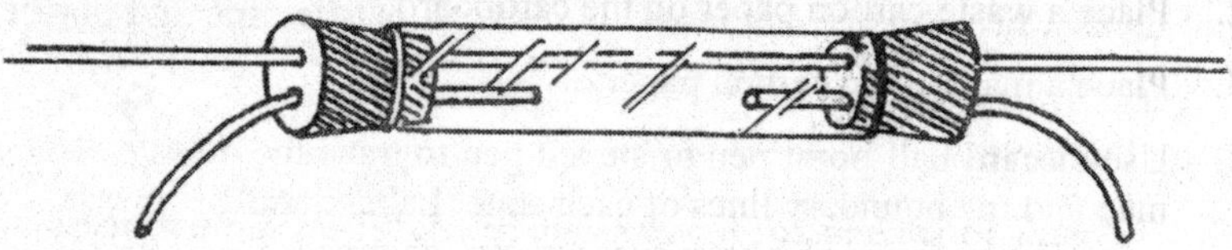

How to Use

To use this condenser, connect the long polythene tubing with the distillation flask tubing. Let the cold water go into one end of the short tubing and out of the other. The circulating cold water will cool the liquid being distilled.

Modification

If polythene (or glass) pipe is not available, a bamboo tube will make a good substitute.

B. MAPS

Brief Description

Maps can be fun with children when they are initiated into map reading and study them very informally. Coloured maps from airline or shipping companies will provide rich learning experiences if the children are permitted to cut them out for puzzles and games or trace the maps for other learning purposes.

Objectives

1. To assist children in recognizing and appreciating shapes of different countries such as the children's own country, the region and the world.

2. To take children on an imaginary tour to different countries.
3. To make inexpensive maps from fun materials.

Materials Used

Two maps (e.g. Malaysia) these may be obtained free of charge from travel agencies, oil companies, high commissions, government departments, etc., stencil pen, scissors, glue, masking tape, cellaphane tape, paper clips, knife and thumbtacks.

How to Make

1. Place a cardboard on the table.
2. Place a waste carbon paper on the cardboard.
3. Place a map on the carbon paper.
4. Use discard ball-point pen or stencil pen to trace the outline of the map and the boundary lines of each state. Label names of the states accordingly. (Now you have a traced outline map).

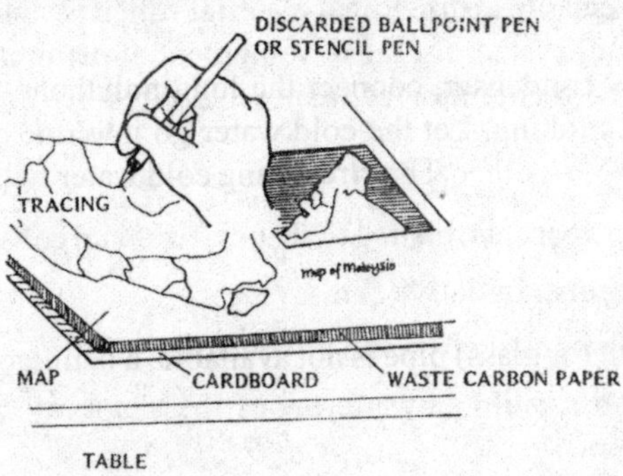

5. Cut the traced outline map.

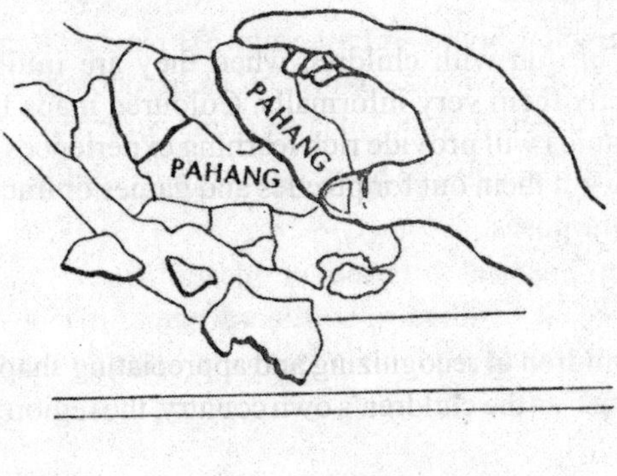

6. Cut out each state from this map by following the boundary lines. (You have a cut-out of the states.) .. cut-outs in a used paper bag.

7. For making an outline map, use an original map (of Malaysia) and ask pupils to cut out the map (of Malaysia) the boundaries. Paste the remainder of the original map on the cardboard. Now you have a blank map (of Malaysia).

How to Use

1. Pupil can have varied matching games by placing each cut-out state on the traced outline map or the blank map.

2. Teacher tells pupil to draw a map without looking at an original map. Label each state on this used cut-out of the states for matching and correction purposes.

C. TANGRAM

1. Brief Description

This is a versatile instructional material which is suitable for all level within the school system for the development of manipulative skills and observation amd recognition of shapes and sizes.

2. Objectives

1. To develop concepts relating to shapes, sizes and conservation of area.
2. To develop manipulative skills.
3. To develop constructive and imaginative ability.
4. To develop a child's awareness of the shape of things in his/her environment.

3. Material Used

- A rectangular board as base (approximately 18 cm X 22 cm) of plywood or other materials such as hardboard, softboard, thick cardboard, scrap wood, plastic, metal sheet, etc.,
- Frame for the sides to hold the tangram (similar materials as the board).
- Tangram material - styrofoam, plasticfoam, rubberfoam, rubber sheets, thick cardboard, softboard, paper-mache, plywood, etc. (material should preferably be easily shaped or cut, and light and durable).

- Hammer, nails, hacksaw, penknife, glue.

4. **How to Make**

1. Prepare a rectangular board (18 cn X 22 cm) using materials suggested above.
2. Cut a small circular hold in the lower half of the board as illustrated, to facilitate removal of the pieces of the tangram from the board.

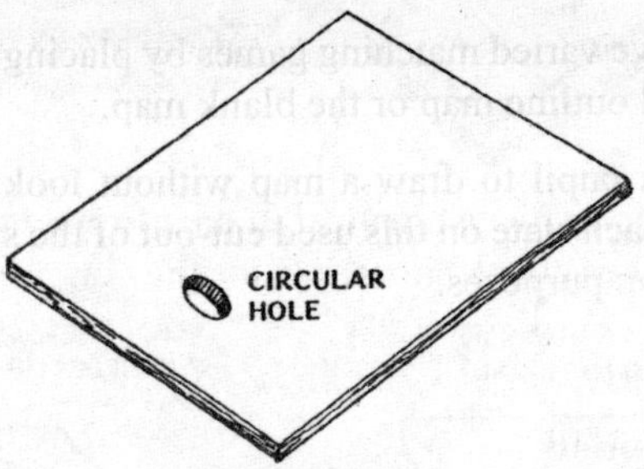

3. Draw a diagram on a piece of paper as shown below.

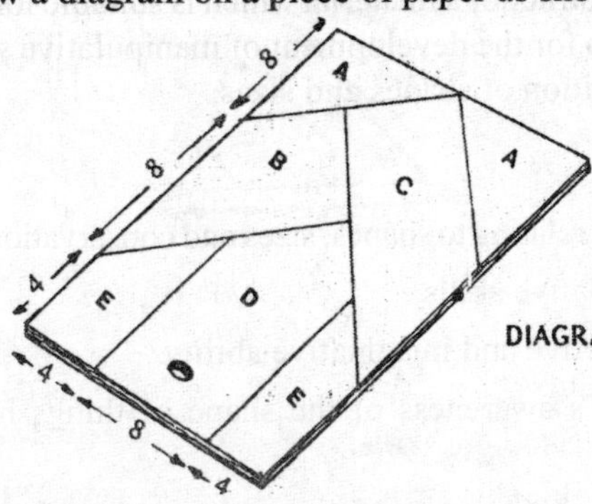

DIAGRAM ON THE PAPER

4. Stick the diagram on the board.

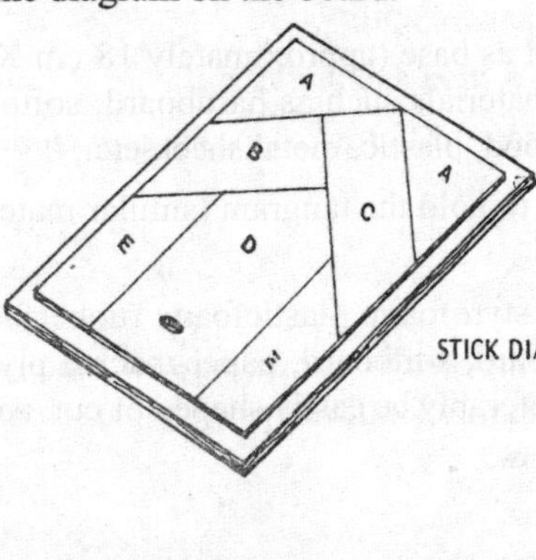

STICK DIAGRAM ON THE BOARD

5. Make a frame using either nails or glue strips of materials similar to that of the board.

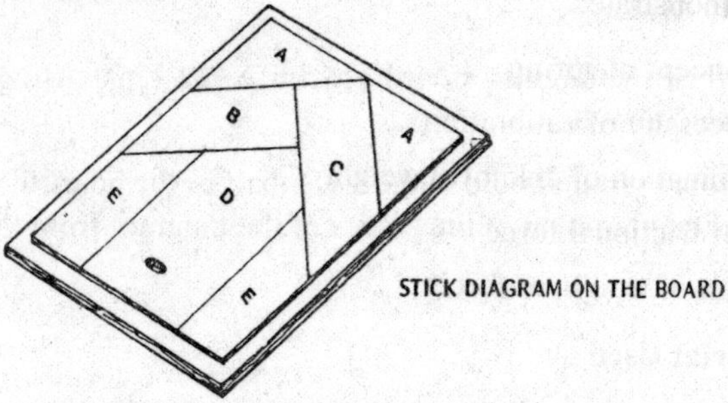

6. Cut a rectangular piece identical in area to the inside of the board. (Use one of the selected materials for the tangram)

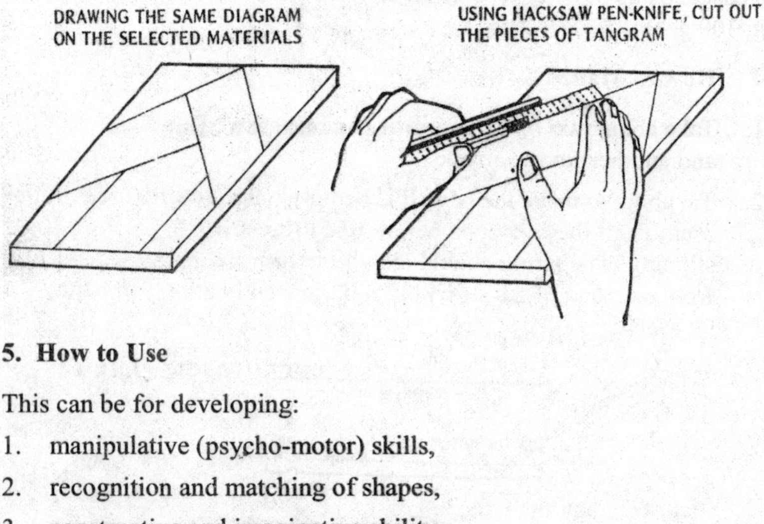

5. How to Use

This can be for developing:

1. manipulative (psycho-motor) skills,
2. recognition and matching of shapes,
3. constructive and imaginative ability,
4. concept of shapes, sizes, area and angles.

Examples of the formulation of different shapes are given below:

D. Spring Balance (II)

1. Brief Description

This is a simple and inexpensive instructional material made of bamboo strips, wire and mesh wire for developing simple science concepts. It looks like a bow and arrow.

2. Objectives

To demonstrate:

1. the concept of spring
2. the necessity of calibration
3. determination of unknown weight
4. idea of frictional force
5. relation of weight to force.

3. Material Used

Strips of bamboo 2.5 cm wide and 0.5 cm thick (or plastic material which can be elastic), lute string, or any other type of string, some wire, a basket made of wiregauze, cane, etc. and standard weight of 100 g, 200 g, 300 g, etc.

4. How to Make

1. Take about two 70 cm length of bamboo strips. Use one for the bow and another for the arrow.
2. Tie about to make the bow. It is better to slightly cut the strip about 3 cm from the two ends before tying the string to prevent it from slipping. The string should also be tied to the arrow about 10 cm from one and of the strip hold it permanently at the centre.

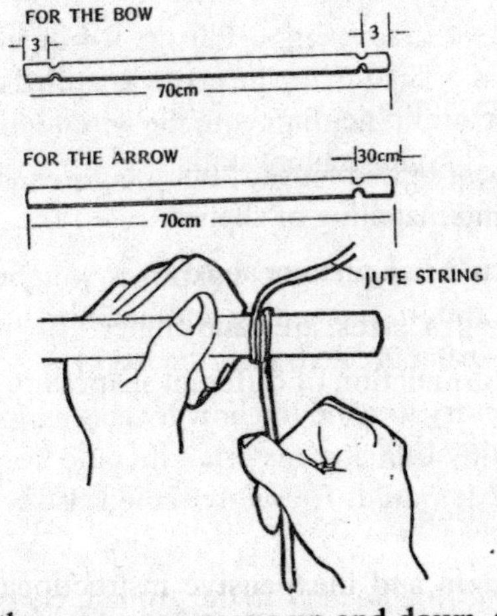

3. In order that the arrow can move up and down, tie the wire around the bow so that it forms a loop.

4. Attach a basket with a nail at the bottom of the arrow.

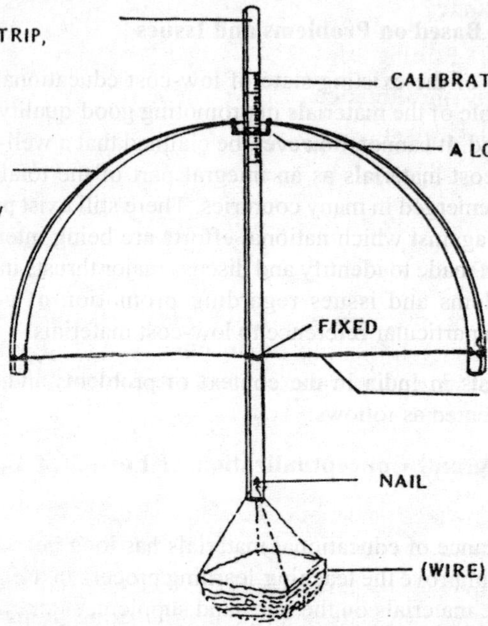

5. How to Use

1. The bow and arrow thus prepared acts as spring balance.
2. Make a mark for zero weight. Put known quantities of weight in steps of 100 gm or 50 gm. As the arrow is pulled dowanwards, mark a line on the arrow coinciding with the wire loop.
3. The scale thus calibrated for say 300-400 gm can now be subdivided into smaller units.
4. It is now ready to determine unknown weights in the range of calibration. (Caution: Exceeding and bending the bow beyond this range may not bring the zero position back)
5. Let the children try to bend the bow by applying their own force. If the bow is made of thicker material, it could be a game to find out the strength of each child. Thus, force could also be measured through weights.
6. Lay down the spring balance on the ground. By tying the bottom of the arrow to a brick or a book/books and making them move on the

same surface, can give an idea of the friction between two surfaces and their relationship with weight and surface area.

Major Thrusts Based on Problems and Issues

The review of the existing state of low-cost educational materials shows that the role of the materials in promoting good-quality education is greatly realized. It cannot, however, be claimed that a well-developed system of low-cost materials as an integral part of the total education process has yet emerged in many countries. There still exist problems of a varied nature against which national efforts are being intensified. An attempt has been made to identify and discuss major thrusts in the region based on problems and issues regarding promotion of educational technology with particular reference to low-cost materials.

Major thrusts in India in the context of problems and issues can broadly be presented as follows:

National Policy and Conceptualization of Low-Cost Educational Materials:

The importance of educational materials has long been recognized in the region to improve the teaching-learning process in the educational institutions. The materials on the one hand supplement and compliment teachers' work in the class room, and arouse pupils' interest and attention on the other. In recent years, there has been a major shift in the national policy towards using aids which are available locally or can be produced cheaply, National policy decisions backed by increasing school populations due to high rates of population growth, together with financial constraints, have led educational institutions to turn to more personal and human teaching by the use of rich natural resources and inexpensive educational materials.

The low-cost educational materials are conceptualized as those which facilitate the learning process and have the following features:

(i) Raw materials easily available from nature and may be directly used as educational aids;

(ii) Simple aids which can be easily prepared from raw materials available from nature, discarded materials or cheap materials from the market; and

(iii) Permanent and durable educational materials (graphic and printed materials, three-dimensional materials, science equipment and kits, audio materials, audio-visual materials, etc.) manufactured locally and which can be procured at comparatively lower costs than sophisticated ones imported from outside.

Under the Serva Shiksha Abhiyan, a flagship programme of the Govt. of India, each teacher at the elementary school level was provided ₹ 500/- for the preparation and use of teaching aids.

One of the major problems encountered in connection with the above is that in some countries the school budget is too small to purchase even low-cost materials and to maintain and replace them when necessary. Furthermore, adequate funds are often not made available to the national institutions to undertake mass production of prototypes developed by them. The fact that the materials so produced are again mostly subject-oriented rather than child-centred poses another big question in the process of purposeful education and development of the child.

Building Up of Infrastructure and Management System

In pursuance of national policy, the Education Department have established some sort of specialized institutions for conducing research, designing, developing evaluating and sometimes mass-producing the suitable prototypes. These apex organizations in many cases take the responsibility for training of teachers and teacher-educators, and distribution and dissemination of materials. Other management activities such as use, storage and maintenance of materials are also pursued by these organizations. But from the viewpoint of physical and financial facilities is far from satisfactory. The institution also suffers from the shortage of a sufficient number of skilled personnel. These organizations often work in isolation 'with little or no co-ordination of activities or interchange of ideas to achieve the common goal of enhancing the quality of education. This issue may be considered important to minimize wastage and calls for immediate attention by all concerned.

Design, Development and Evaluation of Materials

One of the major thrusts noticeable is for the formulation of specific guidelines for design, development and evaluation of low-cost educational materials. An ideal situation which is not present is as follows:

(i) Defining objectives in line with the specific needs of target learners;

(ii) Identifying techniques, raw materials and basic tools needed to achieve the objectives;

(iii) Producing prototypes;

(iv) Trying out prototypes;

(v) Modifying the prototypes where necessary; and

(vi) Finalizing the prototypes for mass production.

Dissemination and Distribution of Materials

Another major thrust for the promotion of low-cost educational materials is to streamline the dissemination and distribution systems of the materials. Functioning of both the systems in an effective manner is considered to be a crucial factor for the success of educational technology programmes. Dissemination of materials is normally done through training programmes, seminars and workshops, publications, exhibitions and displays. There is also a growing trend to use mass media such as radio and television to encourage awareness among users about the significant role of low-cost materials for increasing the quality of teaching techniques and children's learning. However, there still exist national constraints, namely lack of technical know-how, shortage of expertise and trained manpower, inadequate funds and lack of professional commitment by producers and teachers in this regard.

Distribution of the required number of materials to educational institutions at the right time has always been a matter of concern with poor transport and communications. Because of this, rural schools in far-flung areas of the country often get less material support than the rich schools of the urban areas, thus resulting in serious gap in the process of educational development. Although national efforts are geared to facilitate the distribution of materials by the establishment of resource centres at regional and state levels and the involvement of grass-roots level education officers, there still exists room to improve the situation by allowing liberal monetary and manpower support to the concerned agencies.

Involvement of Private and Commercial Agencies in the Promotion of Low-Cost Educational Materials

There is a growing tendency to involve more and more commercial and private organizations to support national activities for the promotion of low-cost educational materials. Private bodies such as civic organizations, science clubs, youth and social clubs, Lions clubs, Rotary clubs, science centres, museums and art galaries are taking an increasing interest in disseminating educational technology among the masses. The role of science clubs in this connection is worth mentioning. Commercial organizations are contributing much to the mass production of a variety of low-cost materials such as maps, charts, globes, models, educational toys and games. Prototypes of science equipment and simple audio-visual aids are also marketed in large numbers by many commercial firms. However, there is no systematic arrangement to ensure quality control of these aids in many countries.

Promotion of Intra- and Inter-Country Exchange of Experiences

Some States have responded in a significant way to the strong initiative for the promotion of educational technology with particular reference to low-cost teaching aids. Participation in these activities has facilitated exchange of experiences in the development of educational materials through discussion, display and demonstration, formulation of general guidelines for the design, development and use of materials and lastly development of examplary materials with standard instruction sheets for national super-visors and teachers.

It may be said that in spite of a major thrust for the advancement of different aspects of low-cost educational technology, the overall situation has not changed much over the years. This is mainly due to national constraints, as follows:

Inadequately-trained teachers, quantity and variety of materials not adequate to meet the growing needs of teachers and curriculum; problems of mass production, distribution, use, maintenance, storage and replenishment of materials; inadequate budget allocation; materials are subject-centred.

Follow Up Actions Required to be planned

A general review of the follow-up actions planned or already undertaken on low-cost educational materials be made in order to develop an insight into the trends and aspirations has been as below :

1. The follow-up actions undertaken or planned may be grouped into six categories: organization of more national seminars, workshops and conferences; exploration of more low-cost educational materials; qualitative and quantitative improvement of teacher orientation and training programmes; dissemination

of low-cost materials by arranging exhibitions and display centres and through the mass media; preparation and distribution of teacher's guides, handbooks and manuals and annotated lists of materials and lastly strengthening of management system in terms of organization, design, development, evaluation, distribution, storage and maintenance.

2. Special emphasis is laid on organization of more seminars, workshops and conferences to facilitate exchange of views and experiences, co-ordinate activities and discuss future lines of action, stress the holding of workshops at both national and regional or provincial levels for the actual development of low-cost educational materials. India attaches importance to the education of key personnel on the value of low-cost materials and developing the competence of the illustrators of educational materials for children through these workshops. Workshop activities, promotion of research and development of material through apex organisations has been stressed.

3. Exploration of new raw materials and innovative low-cost aids is included in the follow-up plan. In India particular reference has been made to educational materials on social sciences, language development of children and special aids for backward areas. Surveys of play material and toys with educational potential are also highlighted. Giving incentives to the producers of best examplary materials by using scrap or local materials is being considered

4. India has planned to provide adequate training to teachers on educational technology with greater emphasis on low-cost teaching aids. It also proposes reorienting the pre-service and in-service training programmes of teachers in order to give more attention to child development through the adequate use of educational technology and through its major programme of Sarve Shiksha Abhiyan.

5. Better use of mass media to promote dissemination of low-cost educational materials are considered to be important in India to revitalize the dissemination process. It is on setting up display centres of low-cost educational materials at state level.

6. Strengthening of management systems to promote low-cost educational materials occupies an important place in the follow-

up plans. It has been proposed to put special effort into consolidating the organizational and logistical aspects of institutions at different levels which are concerned with development and use of low-cost materials. Promotion of functional strategies for design, development and evaluation were also emphasised in the re-orientation proposals of the countries. Other proposals for follow-up action include improvement of storage and maintenance and replenishment facilities for aids, among both producers and users.

Synthesis of Experiences

These is an increasing awareness among the teachers and students about the availability of low-cost materials for the preparation of teaching aids, which can be creatively used to simplify their conceptual problems which they face. There are the problems in design, development utilization and evaluation. There are attitunal problems and constraints such as values of teachers, parents and the community. The teachers feel themselves superior and hesitate to work with the local artisans who can help in the development of working models and toys, etc.

The management of educational materials and the teaching aids is another problem. There are no storage facilities in the elementary schools. At the state and Block/Distt levels there is no mechanism for the dissemination and distribution of low-cost educational material. The educational administration and other agencies for the promotion of these aids hardly evince any interest. Toys and games at local level are of great significance in fostering socio-economic issues.

Suggestions for Future Actions

Synthesis of experiences have elucidated the dimension of programmes embarked on implementation on low-cost educational materials. In physical targets and to some extent in financial terms, achievements in most of the countries appear to be quite appreciable but one must not lose sight of the qualitative aspect. It cannot be claimed that qualitatively the achievement is up to the desired level. No doubt there are big programmes and there is an abundance of low-cost educational materials in some cases, but what next? How can quality be maintained in terms of organization, management, use and professional input? Until and unless these cardinal issues are sorted out and resolved, programmes of low-cost educational materials will hardly bear any real fruit.

Some suggestions are put forward for future action on low-cost educational materials. The proposals are merely suggestive and based on information available in the workshops and case-study reports. The suggestions are discussed in the following paragraphs.

1. ***Strengthen and support more qualitative research***

   More initiative, judgement or educated guesses can no longer be considered sufficient to deal with many intricate aspects of low-cost educational materials in the context of curriculum development such as design, development, use, evaluation and dissemination. This calls for strengthening and supporting more qualitative and problem-oriented research by the concerned institutions and organizations. In this connection training of research workers on low-cost educational technology should receive close attention. Research activities should also be decentralized. For example, in spite of keeping research in the hands of specialized institutions only, teacher-educators and teachers could also be given support to carry out projects.

2. ***Organize more in-service training courses having practical bias on low-cost educational materials***

   Extensive training courses should be conducted for the teachers on educational technology. Besides working teachers, the courses should also occasionally be attended by educational policy-makers, educational administrators and teachers in order to help them develop both an insight into the need for low-cost materials and a positive attitude toward them. Teachers, being the direct users of the materials, should be given a thorough understanding of the relevance, needs, techniques and management aspects (storage, maintenance, exploitation and effective use of local materials and resources involving the guardians; community at large, etc.) of low-cost materials more through demonstrations, field studies and practical sessions. Special inputs should be provided in the courses to arouse their interest in the materials and modify their attitudes to the use of materials in their place of work. Curricula for pre-service training courses should also be modified where needed, so as to give special attention to relevant aspects of educational technology.

3. ***Promote preparation of low-cost aids also on subjects other than science and mathematics***

   In the context of the recent trend to relate low-cost materials mainly to the teaching of Science and Mathematics, it is proposed to focus special attention also on the development and use of low-cost materials for improving the teaching of other subject areas of the curricula, such as languages and Social Studies. Besides strengthening effective teaching of the subjects, this will create a wholesome attitude among all members of the school community towards low-cost educational materials.

4. ***Involve the community and "village technology" to promote the use of low-cost educational materials in the schools***

   Greater involvement of the community, including the parents and guardians of pupils, in supporting academic programmes will greatly facilitate the successful development and use of low-cost educational materials. This can be accomplished by strengthening parent-teacher associations. The co-operation of the parents and community could be sought for supplying raw materials and providing technical know-how available in the villages (termed "Village technology") for the development of the aids. The school authorities could promote their relations with the community by inviting the parents and guardians of the pupils, and community leaders to attend and give all possible assistance to the co-curricular programmes of the schools such as school exhibitions and cultural functions.

5. ***Attach importance to the development and use of pupil-centred materials along with curriculum-centred materials***

   Wholesome development of the child in connection with cognitive psycho-motor, emotional, affective and moral disciplines could be fostered to a great extent by using materials like educational toys, puppets animations and games. So concurrent efforts should be made to develop and use materials both from the curriculum and the children's points of view. However, the utmost care should be taken to design and develop toys and games which are educational, inexpensive, interesting, purposeful, safe to use and not prejudicial to local culture.

6. ***Include educational technology with special emphasis on low-cost materials as an important component of the curricula of teachers' training institutions***

   A well-balanced curriculum of teacher education with special focus on the need for development and use of low-cost educational materials, if implemented properly in the teachers' training institutions, will go a long way to prepare motivated teachers with adequate knowledge and skill to prepare and use inexpensive aids.

7. ***Give due recognition to talented teachers***

With a view to improving attitudes, value and involvement, professional recognition in the form of awards, promotion, salary increments and study-grants should be given to deserving teachers. This could be done by holding regular national competitions on low-cost materials. This will also assist in tapping local talent; such talented people could be given suitable positions in the national institutions to contribute more significantly on low-cost educational technology.

8. ***Prepare national inventories and instructional materials for users of low-cost educational materials***

There is still dearth of teachers' guides, manuals and handbooks in the member countries. Special emphasis should be given to develop these support materials, more suitably in modular form, in adequate numbers and distributing them to teachers. A national inventory with an annotated list of low-cost educational materials with suitable diagrams could prove to be an important resource book for the interested teachers.

Annex I

An abridged list of low-cost, simple educational materials.

Material Classification	Application
(A) Freely-available materials	
(a) Local Environment	
1. **Plant**	
1. bamboo	1. Counting frames: abacus
2. seeds and fruits	2. Mats, display boards
3. weeds and grass	3. Holders
4. leaves, flowers, roots and stems and bark of trees	4. Lettering instruments
5. rice husks and straw	5. Containers

Material Classification	**Application**
6. coconut parts: husks shells sheaves etc.,	6. Musical instruments
7. natural fibres	7. Figurines, models masks, puppet
8. cane	8. Toys and games
9. cotton	9. Simple science apparatus scales, balances, counters
	10. Specimen
	11. Diorama
	12. Suffings of toys and puppets
	13. Aquarium
	14. Terrarium
2. Animal-Insect	
1. shells, corals	1. Specimens
2. insects	2. Figurines and models
	3. Toys and games
	4. Counting aids
	5. Lettering and instruments
	6. Brush
	7. Mobiles and displays
	8. Musical instruments
	9. Weather measuring instruments: humidity indicators, wind vane
	10. Containers
	11. Modules: science, social studies
	12. Aquarium
	13. Terrarium
3. Mineral	
1. Stones, pebbles	1. Counting aids
2. Clay	2. Specimens and objects
3. sand, soil	3. Models

Material Classification	**Application**
4. limestone, marble	4. Chemicals for laboratory experiments
5. salt	5. Moulds for paper mache
6. oil and by-products	6. Toys and games
7. gas	7. Sand tray presentation
8. iron filling	8. Sand paper
9. liquid: water, soft drinks	9. Aquarium
10. tin	10. Toys

B) Waste Materials (Scraps. Discards)

1. Industrial wastes	1. Laboratory activities
2. scrap wood	2. Figurines, models dolls, puppets, masks
3. packing materials: foam, polysterne, vinyle polythene foil	3. Counting devices
4. cloth scraps	4. Games and toys
5. used wire	5. Electric bell
6. paper/glass/plastic cups	6. Electric meter
7. used electric wire	7. Funnel
8. posters	8. Coil bobbins
9. advertisements materials	9. Spring balance
10. discarded stationary	10. Simple motor
11. discarded parts from simple machines	11. Simple boat
12. broken springs	12. Dynamic trolley
13. tines	13. Weather measuring instruments:rain guage, wind vane
14. disposable syringe needles	14. Expansion apparatus
15. saline bottles regulators and tubes	15. Spirit lamp
16. X-ray form	16. Battery-holders
17. sawdust	17. Simple switches

Material Classification	Application
18. newspapers and magazines	18. Test tubes
19. fused bulbs	19. Burettes
20. bottle caps	20. Posters, Dash cards. picture sheets, work cards, cut-outs.
21. wooden crates	21. Audio distribution system
22. cartoon boxes	22. Relief maps
23. old hack saw blades	23. Papier mache products

Domestic Wastes

1. used paper	1. Posters, flash cards, picture sets work cards, cutouts
2. cardboard	2. Toys and games
3. used clothing	3. Puppets, masks
4. newspaper, magazines, books	4. Papier mache articles
5. bottle caps, lids and corks	5. Study kit for: science. social studies, language, home arts
6. postcards, greeting cards	6. Magnifying glass
7. old calendars	7. Counting devices (abacus)
8. used stamps	8. Triple stand
9. matchboxes, cigarette boxes	9. Dioramas
10. bags, envelopes	10. Scrolls
11. string, twine, cord, sewing threads	11. Slides and transparencies
12. elastic material	
13. bicycle tubes, tyres shocks and other parts	
14. ice-cream sticks	
15. empty spools and reels	
16. containers	
17. buttons	
18. used ball-pens	
19. fused bulbs	

C) Accessible-Available at Little Cost Materials

1. paper, cardboard
2. clips
3. nails. pins. needles. paints
4. glue. adhesive
5. buttons, fasteners
6. crayons, colouring materials, paints
7. simple stationary materials
8. candles and wax
9. screws and bolts
10. plywood
11. plastic sheets and bags
12. fabric materials
13. gunny bags
14. soft board
15. rubber stoppers
16. simple elastic materials
17. synthetic boards
18. foam
19. rubber sheets
20. Styrofoam sheets
21. simple toys
22. toy motors
23. puppets, dolls, masks
24. magnets
25. cartons, boxes
26. egg boxes
27. crates
28. Simple electric wires
29. Charcoal, coal
30. Bamboo strips, mats
31. Specimens, models
32. Ping-pong balls

1. Display boards
2. Carts, maps, posters
3. Puppets, shadow plays
4. Toys and games
5. Dioramas, models
6. Modules
7. Simple science instruments
8. Slides and transparencies

Suggested reading

National Book Trust, India (2001)	Ten Little Fingers
NCERT, New Delhi (1982)	Manual of Low Cost Teaching Aids
NCERT, New Delhi (1982)	UNESCO Case Study on Low Cost Educational Material and Equipment in India.
NCERT (1999)	Teaching Aids in Mathematics.
NCERT (1995)	Mathematic Club Activities.
NCERT (1990-2008)	ETV Programes on Low Cost Teaching Aids (list of 80 programs available with CIET (NCERT).
NCERT (1997-79)	Report of Worship on Low Cost Teaching Organised in MP, Kerela, Maharashtra, Rajasthan and Punjab.
NCERT (Dec. 1983)	Report of Worshop on the Development of Science Equipment from local resources.
Sai Publications Jain colony, Ballabhgarh (2011)	Manual of Low Cost Technological Aids Prof. Harmesh Lal
UNESCO Reg. office, Bangkok	Low-Cost Educational Materials.
UNICEF, 73, Lodhi Estate, Delhi (1984)	Preparation for Understanding.

□

5

FLANNEL BOARD IN EDUCATION

INTRODUCTION

A teaching device that makes learning easier, real, lasting and at the same time entertaining and effective is a valuable instructional tool. Experience shows that flannelgraph is also one of such tools. It helps the teacher present vivid and meaningful association pictures to the class. Graphic and tangible cut-outs stick to the flannel board lending drama, colour, magic, progression and participation and thus resulting in quick association and high retention. This new dimension is appealing to the children and they love it. Educationists have endorsed it as the most useful and dynamic teaching aid.

Only the ingenuity of the teacher is the limit to the usefulness and versatility of the flannelgraph as an auxiliary teaching aid. Its impact and advantages as a teaching aid have not been explored fully in our country.

Because of its effectiveness and inexpensiveness, It is aimed at making this simple teaching tool accessible to all teachers. Once its simplicity in construction and adaptability in instruction is known to all our teachers, it is bound to be one of the most popular teaching tools in our schools.

It is designed to guide and assist our teachers in the preparation of flannel board and its materials and to explain to them, how to apply it with advantage in the teaching of almost all school subjects.

Flannel Board

WHAT, WHY AND HOW

This teaching tool is called by different names:

Visual Board

Flick Board

Slap Board

Felt Board

Choreograph

Video graph

The tool consists of only two parts — a board covered with flannel and objects having fuzzy and napped backing.

The principle involved is the interlocking of fibres of two rough or hairy surfaces, so that the pieces pressed on to a background which is hard and vertical will stay. It can be illustrated on a larger scale by pressing two tooth brushes or hair brushes together, so the bristles interlock. In case of flannelgraph similar principle of friction helps an object to cling to the surface of the board.

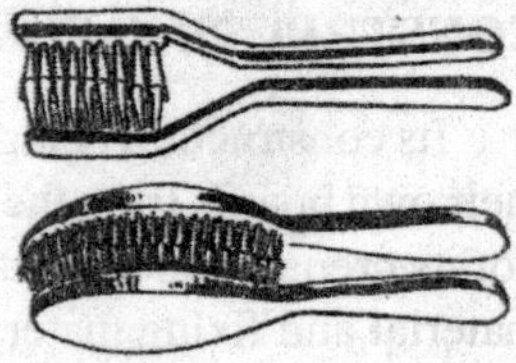

Great interest is aroused when colourful cut-outs stay on the board without the use of any glue, tacks or staples to hold these symbols and pictures. If the flannel is good, the teacher can just flick the illustration on the board where it stays as if by magic. This medium provides ample opportunities to present properly the material without losing the sequence. It increases effectiveness and enables the teacher to remember more of the details. By the dramatic association of pictures and symbols supplemented by teacher commentary, learning interest is heightened and difficult concepts are made easy. It can be used by both the teachers and the pupils, for teaching and learning various skills such as reading, telling stories, giving reports and demonstration, etc.

Its appeal is in the action and suspense. In a way, it is like a drama. It has a story or a plot. It has background or set. It has parts that move about like characters. Like a drama its characters unfold the story before our eyes. The action of moving characters attracts our attention and the suspense of the unfolding story holds our interest.

Not only teachers but even physiotherapists who are interested in simple equipment that can be changed frequently and easily have found flannelgraph as an excellent tool. The patients need no drawing pins or glue or staples to hold the symbols and the pictures.

Flannelgraph can also find a place in the waiting rooms, reception halls and museums where a topical, current and attractive display is wanted.

In teaching, the use of flannelgraph can be made simple as well as elaborate. It may be used to illustrate a difficult point which needs quite a build- up on the board or to highlight a lecture or a speech. Teachers may use it as a means of demonstrating arrangement, to extend concepts and establish visual proof, to provide opportunities in building associations, to enhance dramatic story telling, to stimulate creative expression, to afford means of studying relationships, to provide simple presentation of complicated ideas, to summarise the lesson or the unit and to provide visual type of individual practices. Thus it is almost unrivalled in its use.

CONSTRUCTING FLANNEL BOARDS

Its construction being very simple, many teachers would like to make their own boards from the materials which they can get locally and easily. For its preparation three items are needed, i.e. backing material, covering material and fixing material.

Backing Material: It may be plywood, press board, massonite, wall-board or heavy card board. It must be firm but not too heavy to carry.

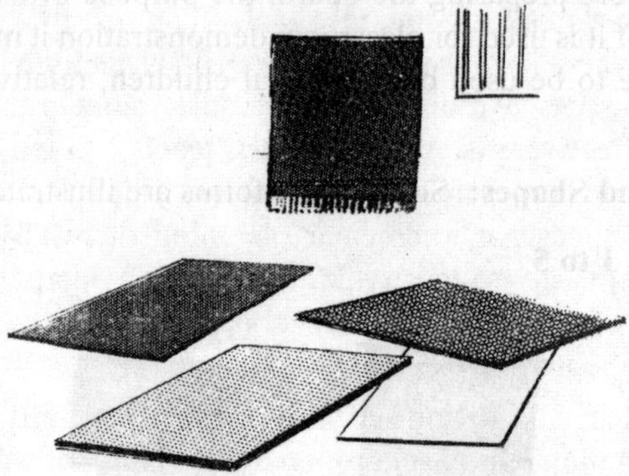

Covering Material: It may be flannel or valour, suede, khadi. Almost any colour can be used but dark-green, black and grey afford excellent contrast for other colours that may be used in presentation.

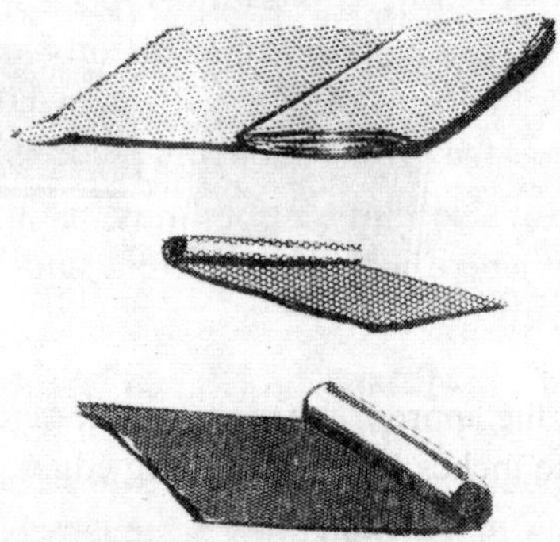

Fixing Material: Rubber cement, tape or staples, nails, thumb tacks, drawing pins, etc. can be used to fix the covering material on the board.

Size: Before preparing the board, the purpose of using it must be kept in view. If it is used for classroom demonstration it may be 4'x5'. If the boards are to be used by individual children, relatively small size would do.

Forms and Shapes: Some of the forms are illustrated here.

Figures : 1 to 5

Construction:

After selecting the appropriate size, cut the selected cloth to fit the board allowing three inches for over-lapping edges.

Stretch the cloth and fasten it tightly with the help of staples or thumb tacks. Be sure that there are no wrinkles on the board because they will cause the material to fall.

In case staples or drawing pins are not available, cloth may be tied with Sutli and needle by catching the edges of the cloth on the back of the board.

In case both sides of the board are to be covered, then two equal pieces of cloth may be cut and the same may be fixed on each side. Three sides may be first sewn and after slipping the board in it, the fourth side may be sewn.

Small individual board may be prepared for children. In nursery classes the top of the biscuit boxes may be covered with flannel or any sensitized material and the box may be used for holding the cut-outs.

Improvising Flannel Boards

A small table or tea-poy may be used with khadi table-cover spread on it.

In a village even a standing charpoy with a blanket or a Khadi bed-sheet spread on it may be used.

Planning, Preparing and Presinting

The technique of making an effective teaching tool is simply the technique of making an experience educationally significant. A prerequisite of every teaching aid is the design of exposition. This design must have organisation and arrangement of ideas, facts and events in a purposeful order. Dewey said "Essential experience has unity". So it is very essential to have proper lay-out prepared and then presented effectively keeping in view the following simple principles of teaching.

1. Simplification

   It shows the ability of the teacher to reach his pupils mentally.

2. Amplification

   It connotes the ingenuity of the teacher to reach his pupils physically. The power of observation is enlarged through amplification.

3. Dramatisation

   Just as simplification of an idea helps to reach the pupils mentally, amplification helps to reach the children physically, dramatisation helps the teacher to reach them emotionally. Emotions are power-ful motors in human machinery

So let us remember these tips for presenting flannel cut-outs:

1. Outline what you want to say.
2. Plan the lay-out keeping in view the principles of teaching.
3. Arrange the materials in such a way that they lend themselves best to illustrate what you want to say.
4. Try the lay-out to see that it fits the space on the flannel board.
5. Place the flannel board at eye-level and at a slightly inclined angle. Lighting should also be checked.
6. Use a minimum number of objects to let the student focus their eyes on a few items at a time.

Work from one side of the board. Stand either on the left or the right side. Avoid to walk in front of the board as it is distracting.

Place the cut-outs on the board carefully but quickly. Take full advantage of the 'MAGIC' or SHOWMANSHIP inherent to flannel board lessons. Don't reveal exactly what the cut-out is, until it is on the board.

Talk to the class as much as possible but not to the board.

Remove the cut-outs from the board as soon as you have finished talking about them and place the next cut-outs in position. It is better to have the interest focussed on one or two cut-outs than to have the attention wandering back to the illustrations already discussed. In case of story-telling or developing a chart, however, the characters might be left on the board.

Visual

It visualizes theoretical ideas.

It helps to recreate situations involving motion.

It visualizes dimensions and colour.

It helps to recreate part.

Audio

It creates events through dramatisation.

It recreates environment.

Utilization

It permits any sequence or arrangement.

It permits restudy.

It permits discussion.

It can be produced locally.

Material For Flannel Board

Nearly all things become visual with the flannel board. Any light weight and flat material can be prepared to adhere on a flannel board. The nap of the flannel board will hold the nap of another piece of flannel placed against it as their fibres interlock. There is a variety of such materials which may be attached to flannel board without using a sensitized backing:

Velore	Balsa wood	Duvetyn or twill
Flannel	Hard Wood	Blotting paper
Felt	Steel Wool	Construction paper
Wool	Velvet	Sand paper
Khadi	Corduroy	Flock paper
Cotton	Cellophane	Emery paper
Suede		

Therefore, object, animals, symbols, numbers, characters, letters, words, musical notes, fractions, circles and various geometrical forms can be cut out of these materials.

In case of children's drawings, tear sheets, pictures, paper cut-outs, title cards, etc. can be displayed on flannel boards by applying a sensitized backing. For this purpose strips of sand paper or flock paper, flannel, khadi or velore may be used with advantage.

Evaluation of Flannelgraph as a Teaching Aid

INTRODUCTION AND STATEMENT OF THE PROBLEM

The purpose of this study is the evaluation of Flannelgraph as a Teaching Aid.

The giant strides taken by some of the nations of the world in the field of Audio-visual Aids are a tribute to their system of education. India cannot afford to sit on the side-lines and be a spectator to this panorama of progress.

To meet the classroom situations as they exist in our country today, it may not be possible for sometimes to equip all our schools with expensive mechanical aids. The accent has to be on in-expensive teacher-made materials which can assist him to communicate better.

Flannelgraph is a simple instructional tool consisting of a nearly vertical surface of flannel and symbols or parts also backed with sand paper or flannel. The flannelgraph works on the principle of friction when parts or objects stick to the cloth of the vertical surface and stay there as if by magic, until they are removed. These associated pictures or symbols help the teachers in the presentation and development of the lesson.

PURPOSE OF THE STUDY

The present investigation was planned to focus specifically upon flannelgraph as a teaching aid and to discover its usefulness for the teaching of Geometry.

REASONS FOR SELECTING GEOMETRY FOR THE EVALUATION OF FLANNELGRAPH

Geometry, perhaps more than any other branch of school mathematics, offers opportunities for attaining all the aims and objectives of teaching mathematics. Plato, a notable, Greek philosopher had an inscription hung over the door of his school entrance, "Let no man ignorant of Geometry enter here". Its power to induce logical thinking prompted Abraham Lincon to carry with him a highly prized volume of Euclid's, Elements.

The concept of size, shape, position and space are extremely necessary to understand the complex nature of what is termed as our rectangular civilization. The study of geometry forms the verb foundation upon which the whole superstructure of engineering, astronomy, physics, architectural drawing and drafting stands because it is the key to mathematical thinking. On the basis of a few maxims and assumptions, a student is able to erect logical structure of established truths, that can be used to discover and prove new facts. It is the 'science of necessary conclusions'. It provides content that ranges from simple to complex and yet it is very objective and non-controversial. It gives ample occasions for exact reasoning, for co-relation with other school subjects such as drawing, geography, algebra and physical sciences, for exercises of space intuition and for training the habits of neatness and exactitude, for the cultivation of the powers of precise thought and accurate expression.

Recent technical advances have placed an increased importance on Geometry of form, size, position, not only in machine shop but also in land scape, architecture, interior decoration and areas of appreciation.

DELIMITATION OF THE PROBLEM

This study delimits to the group which includes lecturers and coordinators of teacher training colleges, principals and teachers from secondary, primary and nursery schools.

The second part of the study concerns the experiment conducted on the students of class IX. The age ranges from 13 to 16 years. They come from lower middle class socio-economic group with their parents income ranging from ₹ 2000 to ₹ 8000.

METHODS AND PROCEDURE

In order to evaluate the effectiveness of flannelgraph for learning as well as for teaching, the study was divided into two parts. The first part was confined to the reactions of the teachers, teaching different school subject at different class levels.

Demonstrations of the use of flannel-graph for the teaching of different school subjects were given to the teachers from the nursery school level to the higher secondary, lecturers from teachers training colleges, teachers from Junior Basic Teacher Training Colleges and also instructors of general education from the field of workers' education, social education, family planning and panchayat raj institutes. These teachers, had represented different states and union territories of India.

T-1 Table Showing the Education Attainment of the Try Out Samples

M.A. AND P.G.B.T.	230
B.A. AND P.G.B.T.	414
MATRIC AND H.S. trained	602
Total	**1246**

T-2 Table Showing the Age Distribution of the Try Out Sample

Above 50 years	150
41 to 10 years	205
31 to 40 years	345
21 to 30 years	390
Below 21 years	156
Total	**1246**

T-3 Table Showing the Socio-Economic States of Try Out Sample

Above ₹ 5000 + allowances	65
₹ 4001 to 5000+ allowances	82
₹ 3001 to 4000 + allowances	125
₹ 2001 to 3000 + allowances	354
₹ 1000 to 2000 + allowance	620

T-4 Table Showing the Number if Teachers at Different Levels

Nursery School Teachers	120
Primary School Teachers	552
Secondary School Teachers	264
Teachers Training College Lecturers end Coordinators	40
Instructors engaged in General education	270
Total	**1246**

T-5 Table Showing the Number of the Instructors in Different Fields of General Education

Panchayat Raj Instructors	44
Social Education Officers	82
Block Development Officers	21
Medical Social Workers	66
Family Planning Doctors and Doctors engaged in Community medicine from Punjab	57
Total	**270**

T-6 Table Showiing the Period Covered for Try Out Sample

1991-92	256	teachers
1992-93	304	-do-
1993-94	506	-do-
1994-95	121	-do-
1995-96	59	-do-
	1246	

Contents of the Flanneigraph Demonstration

1. Preparation and use of various types of flannel boards.
2. Preparation and use of symbols pictures and objects.
3. Flannelgraph for the teaching of Hindi, English, Mathematics, Social Sciences, Health and Hygiene, Psychology, General Science.

After the demonstration the reactions of the teachers were taken through a questionnaire Spot light on the use of flannelgraph as a teaching. It was a short questionnaire and the teachers were asked to give their views frankly.

They were told that they need not mention their names. The total number of teachers investigated from 1991 to 1996 February was 1246. They were told to underline the appropriate symbol (letter) indicating their rating. The data collected has been given below.

SYMBOLS –

L - of little use

C - of considerable use

E - of extreme use

DATA COLLECTED

1. REACTIONS OF THE NURSERY SCHOOL TEACHERS AND PRINCIPALS

L 2

C 19 Total No. 120

E 99

2. Reactions of the Elementary School Teachers and Principals

L 11

C 47 Total No. 552

E 494

3. Reactions of the Secondary School Principals and Teachers

L 79

C 121 Total No. 264

E 64

4. Reaction of Lecturers and Coordinators from Teacher Training Colleges

L 3

C 26 Total No. 44

E 15

5. Reaction of Instructors from Social Education Centres

L	30	
C	169	Total No. 270
E	71	

T-7 Table Showing the Rating of the Elementary Teachers for the Teaching of Different School Subjects

Subiect	L	C	E
English	78	94	380
Language skills	110	150	292
Arithmetic	118	174	260
Social Studies	72	151	319
General Science	101	281	170

T-8 Table Showing the Rating of the Secondary School Teachers for Teaching Different School Subjects

Subjects	L	C	E
English	44	134	86
Mathematics	84	136	44
Science	131	90	43
Social Studies	101	102	61

T-9 Table Showing the Rating of Instructors of General Education

	L	C	E
For giving information	30	169	71
For building attitudes	49	170	5
For imparting education	41	179	170

T-10 Table Showing the Consolidated Rating by The Teachers of Different Levels

L	125	
C	375	Total No. 1246
E	743	

T-11 Table Showing the Reaction of Male and Female Teachers

	MALE	FEMALE
L	76	49
C	199	183
E	298	445

T-12 Table Showing the Calculated Data About the Reachtion of the Teachers

	REACTIONS		L	C	E	Chi-square	Significance level at .01 or .001
A	Reactions of the Nursery school teachers & principals		2	19 120	99	134.14	Yes
B	Reactions of Elementary school teachers & Principals		11	47 552	494	787	"
C	Reactions of Secondary school teachers & Principals		79	121	64	19.8	"
D	Reactions of lecturers and Corrdinators of teachers Training Colleges		3	26 44	15	18	"
E	Reactions of Instructors of General Education		30	169 270	71	113.3	"
F	Subject-wise rating by Elementary School teachers						
	English		78	94	350	313.0	"
	Language skills		110	150	292	99.4	
	Arithmetic		118	174	260	61.2	"
	Social Studies		72	161	319	166.9	"
	General Science		101	281	170	89.6	"
G	Subject-wise rating by secondary school teachers						
	English		44	134	89	46	
	Mathematics		84	136	44	40.4	
	Science		131	190	43	44	
	Social Studies		101	102	61	12.4	
H	General & consolidated reactions by teachers		125	378	743		"
I	Reactions of Male and	Male	76	199	298	129.4	"
	Female teachers	Female	49	183	445	359	"

T-13 Table showing factors of Educational Potentiality of Flannelgraph with Frequency Percentage

S. No.	Factors	Frequency %
1.	Helps to teach better	76.3%
2.	Economises time	56.5%
3.	Helps to teach effectively	86%
4.	Affords opportunities to integrate learning	66.4%
5.	Helps to accomplish more in less time	68.2%
6.	Creats interest to prove action	63.4%
7.	Enriches the teacher and the learner	62.3%
8.	Emphasises relationship	52.2%
9.	Fosters realisation of abstract concepts	64.2%
10.	Lessens verbalism	62%
11.	Identifies facts & figures	63%
12.	Visualizes basic concepts	82%
13.	Vividifies teaching	79%
14.	Provides happy learning	75%
15.	Tells the lesson more forcefully	63%
16.	Provides equality of opportunity	62.5%
17.	Encourages further interest in learning	44.1%
18.	Gives association and Co-relation	49.2%

The second part of the study was a small experiment taken with the mathematics students of class IX. Sixty students of Class IX were selected from four different schools of Vinay Nagar area at Sarojini Nagar Government Boys Higher Secondary School on 1 February, 1996. Before starting the experiment the group as a whole was given a test in Geometry on the basis of their achievement — two matched groups were formed. The age of students ranged from 13 to 15. They were from almost similar socio-economic group. The maximum marks allotted for the test were 50.

T-14 Table Showing the Records of the Students in Geometry Before the Experiment

Controlled Group		Experimental Group	
Roll Nos.	Marks obtained	RollsNos.	Marks obtained
5	35	16	34
15	33	4	33
17	30	1	31
2	30	11	31
13	27	6	26
27	27	3	26
7	25	49	26
10	25	23	26
22	20	13	25
24	26	47	75
22	20	28	20
43	20	44	20
19	20	20	20
51, 54, 59	20, 25, 24	60, 52, 53	22, 22, 22
59, 55, 57	22, 20, 20	58, 56	21, 20
50	18	26	18
46	18	28	18
39	20	45	18
35	18	28	18
31	15	25	16
48	15	40	16
38	15	41	15
34	15	37	15
42	15	30	15
9	10	32	10
12	10	14	10
21	5	36	5

The students had not learnt circle and related theorems. Usually, this unit is covered in the beginning of Class X in Delhi Schools.

Keeping this fact in view the investigator had designed special flannelgraph kit. "On teaching circle and its related theorems through flannel-graph". This kit was developed in consultation with an experienced school principal (Dr. D.P. Singh) who had 15 years experience of teaching mathematics.

The controlled group was taught the following basic definition and one theorem based on circle:

BASIC DEFINITION:

Circle	-	Radius	Sector - Concentric circles
Diameter	-	Segment	Chord - Arc Quadrant
Major Segment	-	Secant	Tangent

Theorem Based on Circle

A straight line drawn from the centre of a circle bisecting chord, which is not a diameter is at right angle to the chord.

The method of teaching the controlled group was the usual maths prevalent in schools. Chalk board and compass were freely used to illustrate the lesson.

The experimental group was taught the same definitions and theorem with the help of flannel cut-outs which were specially prepared for this purpose. Both these groups were taught by the investigator here in the present of 54 mathematics teachers from different schools Zone II, under the Directorate of Education, Delhi Administration.

The time conusmed with the chalk board technique was the whole period of 40 minutes but with the flannel-graph cut-outs the whole matter covered in 22 minutes. The remaining time was spent for re-enforcing the matter covered. So the time given to both the groups was 40 minutes.

After covering both the groups the students were told to go back to their own schools and come thereafter five days. The teachers were retained by the investigator. They were told that in evaluation the worth of a visual aid of the kind under review, there are two aspects which have to be taken into consideration.

1. The subject matter, i.e. the content of the lesson or the unit which is to be taught.

2. The method and the material which present the matter. It is important to know how far this aid has helped in reducing the effort and the time involved on the part of the learner for understanding it and the teacher for teaching it. Keeping these two aspects into consideration, a simple set of straight forward and specific questions was devised. The purpose of those questions was to get the judgement of the teachers who are to use it. The answer to these questions, spotlighted the features of this particular aid and also helped in interpreting their judgements quantitatively and thus to gauge the extent to which further improvement is desirable. The questions also acted as safeguard against personal prejudices and hasty judgements. A three-point scale was devised for comparing its effectiveness on objective basis and thus reducing the subjectivity to a great extent. The points given in the scale from l to 3 means measuring the visual aid in respect of usefulness, i.e.

Symbols

1. To a large extent — L
2. To some extent — S
3. To no extent — N

T-15 Items Wise Rating by the Teachers

Item	Question	L	S	N
1.	Do you feel that this kit has clarified the concepts which were required to be taught in this unit?	49	3	2
2.	Does this kit help the teacher and the children in providing organised material to develop following up activities for preparing such cut outs for reforcing what has been taught?	47	4	3
3.	Does this kit stimulate thinking on the part of the learners?	28	20	6
4.	Do you feel that this kit can prove as a supplementary aid for teaching Geometry?	28	24	2
5.	Do you think that these ready-made cut outs can help in reducing the time required for teaching this unit?	32	15	7
6.	Do you think that these ready made cut outs can help in reducing the effort required for the teaching of this unit?	31	21	2
7.	To what extent do ybu think this kit can stimulate the children to make thier own cut-outs for reenforcing their learning?	22	20	12
8.	A satisfactory aid has to embody all the syllabi details of the unit under study. Does this kit attended to such details in the unit "Circle and related theorems?	31	19	4

9.	A Visual aid is stated good if it helps not only the bright pupils but also the children of different levels of ability?	31	19	4
10.	Do you think that this kit can interest the children by bringing colour magic, drama participation and progression in the class?	49	4	1
11.	Do you think that this kit can help the children to widen their horizon and increase their imagination in using geometrical cut-outs?	47	4	3
12.	Do you think that it can help the student recall or apply the knowledge gained?	41	9	4
13.	Do you feel that the material in this kit is adaptable and the teacher can present the material, in the way he likes and at any time of need?	29	21	4
14.	Do you think that this kit can be used and preserved for many years?	39	10	5
15.	Does this kit provide material for coorelation and activity for the teaching of related materials?	21	17	16

EDUCATIONAL POTENTIALITY OF THE ITEMS IN THE QUESTIONNARIES

All the questionnaires which were distributd to the teachers at various stages of this study had 45 to 60% of the items regarding curricular content and 40 to 55% of the items about the presentation of the content. The last questionnaire which was distributed to the teachers to evaluate the effectiveness of the flannel kit for teaching "Circle and related theorems" the ratio of responses is given below:-

T-16 Table Showing the Educational Potentiality of the Items

	Raw score			Calculated data	
Area	L	S	N	Chi-square	Significance
(i) Curricular content	279	103	40	214.7	Highly significant
(ii) Method and material	310	143	42	210.3	-do-

Final Rating

After a lapse of five days group, i.e. Experimental group and the Control group were given a short objective type test - see Appendix IV.

Given below are the tables of raw score and calculated data:-

T-17 Table Showing the Raw Score of the Controlled and Experimental Groups

Experimental Group			Controlled Group		
Score	Frequency	fx	Score	Frequency	fx
60	7	420	60	2	120
55	12	660	55	2	110
50	6	300	50	2	100
40	1	45	45	1	45
40	1	40	40	4	160
35	1	35	35	2	70
30	2	60	30	2	60
	No. 30		25	3	75
			20	8	160
			25	4	60
				No. 30	

Efx = 1560

Arithmetic Mean = Efx/No

1560 x 1/30 = 52

Ef x = 960

Arithmetic Mean = Efx/No

961 x 1/30 = 32

T-18 Table Showing the Calculated Data of TheTwo Groups

Experimental Group

Original Data			Calculated Data			
X	F	FX	d	fd	fd²	
60	7	420	8	56	408	Standard Deviation
55	12	660	2	36	108	
50	6	300	–2	–12	24	$\sqrt{\frac{fd^2}{No}}$
45	1	45	–7	–7	49	$\sqrt{\frac{990}{30}}$
40	1	40	–12	–12	144	= 8.1
35	1	70	–17	–17	289	
30	2	60	–22	–44	968	

Controlled

Original Data			Calculated Data			
X	F	FX	d	fd	fd²	
60	2	120	28	56	1568	Standard deviation
55	2	110	23	46	1058	$\sqrt{\frac{fd^2}{No}}$
50	2	100	18	36	648	
45	1	45	18	13	169	$\sqrt{\frac{6180}{30}}$
40	4	160	8	32	256	
35	2	70	3	6	18	14.3
30	2	60	–2	–4	8	
25	3	75	–7	–21	147	
20	8	160	–12	–96	1152	
15	4	60	–17	–68	1156	

Graphic Representation of the Score

Experimental Group

----

15 20 25 30 35 40 45 50 55 60

Graphic Representation of the Score

Controlled Group

15	20	25	30	35	40	45	50	55	60

The statistical analysis of the data (Airthmetic mean and Standard Deviation) was very revealing. The arithematic mean of the Controlled group was 32 and that of the Experimental group was 52. Apparently, the difference between the two means was so great that no need was felt to go into the further analysis of the data for its significance.

Table Showing Contingency Coefficient Between the Educational Attainment and the Frequencyt Response of the Teachers

Qualifications	L	C	E
M.A.P.C.B.T. TEACHERS	46	121	64
B.A.B.T. TEACHERS	131	114	170
Materic & Hr. Sec Trained Teachers	56	240	315

Contingency co-efficient was calculated. It came out to be. 73 which is very significant. It shows evidently that there is a close correlation between the educational attainments of the teachers and the use of flannelgraph for teaching.

SUMMARY OF THE PROCEDURE FOLLOWED

In order to map out the educational potentiality of fennelgraph as a teaching aid, sample teachers from different levels of instruction and from different parts of India were given demonstrations about the use of flannelgraph in instruction.

For determining the educational potentiality of flannelgraph a list of factors constituting the values of flannelgraph as a teaching aid was drawn up in consultation with five prominent teachers. This list of factors was converted into a form of a questionnaire.

After the demonstrations, the reactions of the teachers were taken through a questionnaire "Spot light on the use of flannelgraph as a teaching aid"

Reactions to both the questionnaires were collected and calculated. In the end their significance level was discovered.

Almost same procedure was followed with Part II of the study. Test scores of the Experimental and the Control groups were calculated.

Regarding the evaluation of the flannel kit on teaching "Circle and related theorems" another questionnaire was distributed to the teachers after its demonstrative use with the Experimental group in the present of 52 teachers of Mathematics in Sarojini Nagar Govt. Boys Hr. Sec. School No. 2 on 2.2.1966. The reactions of the teachers were calculated.

In order to find out the co-relation between two different sets of alternatives, the Contingency Coefficient method wan used.

In this Study, the measurement consists in assessing teachers responses to a set of questions. Each particular question which evoked the response has been called on "items: The question; Do you think that these readymade cutouts can help in reducing the time required for teaching this unit", together with a three point responsible, (L) — to a large extent, (S) to some extent, (N) to no extent constitutes an item. The number assigned to an individual's item response is an item score that gave the weightage assigned to each response.

Regarding "measurement" there are different methods of measuring score but method of Rank Order scale was selected investigator as it is a popular and the most practical of all psychometric methods.

FRAMING OF ITEMS

Teachers and Principals were consulted for the preparation of the items. Effort was made to give 50% of weightage to the curricular content and 50% to the method of presentation. It has been statistically proved — refer to Table no. 16.

Arithmetic mean was taken up as the most reliable vital point. This mean is the "Fulcrum" or balance of forces in a see-saw. It is that point of true equilibrium of the sum of moments on the two sides. These moments are determined by both, i.e. distance from the fulcrum and the weight of the cases scattered a long see-saw. In a range of score from high to low with a number of cases making a score which is called frequency distribution.

RELIABILITY

Factors which attribute towards the reliability of this study are:

I. (a) Identity of the group.

(b) Uniformity of instructions to both the groups.

(c) Identify of the physical and mental conditions of the testees as far as possible.

II. Used Chi-square method and found significance level.

III. Used contingency co-efficient, i.e. the sum of the methods in non-parametric statistic where the distribution is not normal.

VALIDITY

For the validity of the questionnaire, it was assumed that they assessed the attitudes of the teachers towards the use of flannelgraph in teaching. The respondents 1245 in the first part of the study and 53 teachers in the second part of the study felt that the questionnaires were relevant.

In addition to this test the questionnaires were considered valid. The method of determining validity was to see that the test is related with some accepted way of measuring the achievement of the pupils. Test scores of the two groups and the significance level of the teachers mark a definite claim for its validity.

Conclusion

As the present study was divided into two parts, the conclusions derived from each one have been given below separately.

In part I, the study was confined to 1246 teachers teaching at different levels of instruction, from different parts of India Tables (1,2,3,4 and 5). They were given demonstrations about the preparation and use of flannelgraph for teaching different subjects at different levels. After demonstrations, their reactions were noted with the help of questionnaire (only summary form). They significantly favour the use of flannelgraph as a teaching aid. The calculated data evidently snows the same Tables 7,8,9.10,11 and 13.

These groups of teachers were covered by the investigator, as and when they came to the Depth of Teaching Aid for training or for certain ad hoc lectures. So it took a long time.

Reactions of male and female teachers are also very revealing. It shows that female teachers are more inclined for the use of flannelgraph (Table 11).

Reactions of nursery & elementary school teachers are significant as compared with the secondary school teachers (Tables 10 and 13).

Calculations indicate that flannelgraph is more suited for some subjects at Secondary and Elementary levels than others (Table 13).

Part II of the study was concerned with the experiment. Here 60 students of Class IX were collected. They were divided into two matched groups. (Table 14). The controlled group was given a Geometry lesson on circle and its related theorems. The method of teaching was the usual way of teaching. Chalk board and compass were amply used. The Experimental group was given the same lesson with the help of flannel-graph cut-outs. These lessons were given by the investigator in the presence of 52 teachers from different schools.

After the demonstrative use of flannelgraph, a questionnaire was given to the teachers. The reactions of the teachers were recorded and calculated. They significantly favoured the use of flannel- graph.

The questionnaire contained 45% of the items about curricular content and 55% about the material and method of presentation. These two sets of factors helped the investigator to find out the educational potentiality of the items.

After five days, the same groups of students were given an objective type test.

The analysis of the data was very revealing for raw score and for calculated score. Their achievements have also been shown graphically.

The arithmetic mean of the Controlled group was 32 and for the Experimental group was 52. Apparently, difference between the two means was so great that no need was fine to go into the further analysis of the data for its significance. The calculated score of the Experimental group significantly favours the use of flannelgraphs as a supplementary aid.

Educational potentiality of flannelgraph as an assistant to teach better and effectively, to identify facts, to vividify teaching, to visualize basic concepts, to foster realization of abstract ideas, etc. is highly revealing.

Summary and Suggestions

Audio-visual Aids have been widely recognised in any progressive system of education, yet their suitability or educational value remains unexplained in a strictly scientific sense in our Indian conditions.

This study is an attempt to investigate and measure the educational potentiality of flannelgraph as a teaching aid.

Effort has been made in this study to explore the suitability and educational potentiality of flannelgraph as a teaching aid at different levels of instruction for teaching different school subjects.

This study has also considered its suitability, as to this extent it can arouse and sustain interest of the children and adults, the extent to which its use can be spread over at different levels and to the extent to which academic knowledge can be imparted through it.

The investigation has been carried out in three stages:

(i) Giving demonstration to teachers of different levels of instructions and accqainting them with the potentiality of this flannelgraph.

(ii) Collecting reactions about its potentiality and analysing them statistically.

(iii) Experimental study of its use for teaching Geometry to Class IX, for which a special kit was designed and which has been evaluated by 52 mathematics teachers.

The work of systematically explaining the educational possibilities of flannelgraph is quite new. There seems to be little work doing in this direction even in advanced countries where educational research has taken long strides.

Since fresh ground has been broken, the work has been done in exploratory way and should be followed suit by exploratory attempts.

APPENDIX I

Spot Light on the Use of Flannelgraph in Teaching

(Only in summary form)

We would like to ask you a few questions about your observations and reactions regarding the use of flannelgraph in teaching. Kindly place a check before each response below, that applies in your case:

1. What is your general opinion about flannelgraph as a teaching aid?

   Very much ☐ good ☐ poor ☐

2. Do you think that flannelgraph can arouse and sustain interest of the learners?

   very much ☐ much ☐ very little ☐

3. In case you are an elementary or nursery school teacher

Do you think that flannelgraph can be helpful to you for teaching following subjects:

(a) English ☐ Little ☐ Some ☐ Much ☐

(b) Math ☐ Little ☐ Some ☐ Much ☐

(c) Social Studies ☐ Little ☐ Some ☐ Much ☐

(d) Language Skills ☐ Little ☐ Some ☐ Much ☐

(e) General Science ☐ Little ☐ Some ☐ Much ☐

(In case you are a second school teacher)

4. Do you think that flannel-graph can be helpful to you for teaching following subjects:

(a) English ☐ Little ☐ Some ☐ Much ☐

(b) Mathematics ☐ Little ☐ Some ☐ Much ☐

(c) Social Studies ☐ Little ☐ Some ☐ Much ☐

(d) Home Science ☐ Little ☐ Some ☐ Much ☐

(e) Science ☐ Little ☐ Some ☐ Much ☐

(f) Agticulture ☐ Little ☐ Some ☐ Much ☐

(g) Languag ☐ Little ☐ Some ☐ Much ☐

5. (In case you are an instructor or coordinator in teacher training institutes).

Do you think that flannelgraph can assist you in communication.

Very much ☐ Much ☐ Little ☐

6. (In case you are a teacher engaged in general education) Do you think that flannelgraph can assist you for the following jobs:-

(a) To impart information ☐ Yes ☐ No

(b) To educate ☐ Yes ☐ No

(c) To change attitudes ☐ Yes ☐ No

Kindly give your particulars also.

Name________________Sex ____________

Address___________________________________(State)__________

Level of teaching (check one)

1. Nursery school
2. Slenntary School
3. Secondary school
4. Teachet Training College
5. Instructors in Social & General Education
6. Any other category

Please tick 'Yes' or 'No'.

S.No.	Statements	Yes	No
1.	It has helped to teacher. Better and more effectively.		
2.	It has economised time.		
3.	It has made teaching effective.		
4.	It has not afforded opportunities to integrate learning.		
5.	It has helped to add meaning and significance to verbal symbols.		
6.	It has not helped to accomplish more in less time.		
7.	It has creased interest to provoke action.		
8.	It has enriched the teacher and the learner.		
9.	It has encouraged further interest in learning.		
10.	It has emphasized relationships.		
11.	It has fostered realisation of abstract concepts.		
12.	It has given association and correlation.		
13.	It has lessened verbalism.		
14.	It has identified facts and figures.		
15.	It has provided an unhappy learning.		
16.	It has helped to retain less in more time.		
17.	It has hold the story more forcefully.		
18.	It has not visualised basic concepts.		
19.	It has vivid teaching.		
20.	Teachers would be happy to use more of such teaching kits.		

EVALUATION EFFECTIVNESS OF A FLANNELGRAPH KIT "TEACHING CIRCLE AND RELATED THEOREMS"

The worth of a visual aid of this kind under review, there are two aspects which have to be taken into consideration:

1. The subject-matter, i.e. the content of the lesson or the unit which is to be taught.
2. The method and the material which present the matter. It is important to know how far this aid has helped in reducing the effort and the time involved on the part of the learner for understanding it.

   Keeping these two aspects into consideration, a simple set of straight forward and specific questions has been devised. The purpose of these questions is to get the judgement of the teachers who are to use it. The answer to these questions will not only spotlight the features of this particular aid, but will also will help the institute in interpreting their judgements qualitatively and thus to gauge the extent to which further improvement is desirable. These questions would also act as safeguard against personnel prejudices and hasty judgements. A three-point scale suggested below will provide the institute with a statistical answer for comparing its effectiveness on objective basis and thus reduce the subjectivity to a great extent. The points given in the scale from 1 to 3 mean measuring the visual aid in respect of its usefulness, i.e.

   1. To a large extent
   2. To some extent
   3. To no extent

S. No.		To a large extent	To some extent	To no extent	Weight by the Reviewer
1.	Do you feel that this kit has clarified the concepts which were required to be taught in this unit?				
2.	Has this kit helped the teacher and the children in providing organised material to develop				
	a) Basic concepts				
	b) Acquaintance with these figures				
	c) Follow-up activity for preparing such cut-outs for reinforcing what has been taught or for applying the information				
3.	Did this kit stimulate thinking on the part of the learner?				
4.	Do you feel that this kit can prove as a supplementry aid for teaching geometry?				
5.	Do you feel that these readymade cut-outs have helped you in reducing the time required for teaching the unit?				
6.	Do you think that these readymade cut-outs have helped you in reducing the effort required for teaching this unit?				
7.	To what extent do you think that this kit has motivated the children to make their own cut-outs for reinforcing their learning?				
8.	A satisfactory aid has to embody all the syllabi details				

S. No.		To a large extent	To some extent	To no extent	Weight by the Reviewer
	of the unit. Has this kit attended to such details in the unit "Circle and Related Theorems"?				
9.	A visual aid is rated good if it helps not only the bright pupils but also the pupils of average ability in the class. Do you think that this kit will be helpful to the children of different levels of ability?				
10.	Has this kit interesting children by bringing (a) Color, (b) Magic, (c) Drama, (d) participation, (e) progression in the classroom?				
11.	Has this kit help the children to widen their horizon and increase their imagination in using geometrical cut-outs?				
12.	will it help the students in recalling or applying the knowledge gained?				
13.	Do you feel that the material in the kit is adaptable and the teacher can present the material in a way he likes, at any time of the year?				
14.	Do you think that this kit can be used and peserved for many years?				
15.	Does this kit provide material for corelation and activity for the teaching of related materials?				

S. No.		To a large extent	To some extent	To no extent	Weight by the Reviewer
16.	The estimate of cost is very important for the school. Will the school be in a position to meet the cost of such educational kits?				
17.	Would you like to assist this institute in developing more of such kits, for the teaching of Algebra, Geometry, Arithmetic, as educational consultants?				
18.	How would you rate this kit in general?				

Particulars of the Evaluation

Name (in Block Letters):____________________________________

Designation and Address:____________________________________

Academic qualifications:____________________________________

Experience in the field of teaching Mathematics_____________

APPENDIX II

TWELVE ITEM CONCEPT TEST

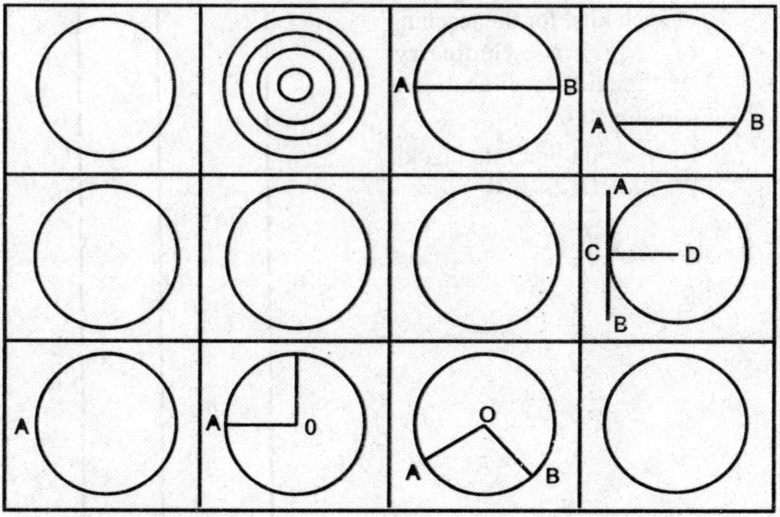

1. CHORD
2. QUADRANT
3. MINOR SEGMENT
4. SECTOR
5. SECANT
6. RADIUS
7. MAJOR SEGMENT
8. CONCENTRIC CIRCLE
9. TANGENT

10. CIRCLE
11. SEMI-CIRCLE
12. DIAMETER

INSTRUCTION: Recognise the figures in the square and give them names of numbers.

□

6

(A) DEVELOPING LEARNING MATERIAL FOR LITERACY AND CONTINUING EDUCATION

These days much stress is being laid on spreading literacy and organising continuing education programmes for adult learners. In both these endeavours follow-up cf the learners becomes very important. They should be provided a variety of material—both print and non-print—not only to sustain their interest but also for giving them information useful for their life needs. In the present article the author has underlined the role of audio-visual learning materials in this context.

Literacy programme has been in existence for over 48 years in this country but the limited impact it has had, indicates that there are some basic problems which need to be identified and understood. The basic problem may be in terms of motivation and the long-term interest of the learners, methodology of teaching, the kind and the quality of educational materials for teachers and learners and perhaps many more. Other problems relate to evolving alternative strategies for curriculum development, preparation of teaching aids, evaluation and follow-up. These problems may differ from one part of the country to another.

There has been an unprecedented growth of population and expansion of knowledge and along with this there has been a substantial increase in the number of schools but even this number has been offset by the explosion of population. New methods and materials have not kept pace with the tremendous explosion of knowledge in technological, scientific and other areas. There is a problem being faced because of the heavy rate of drop-outs and those who never enter the school. It is thus obvious that education can no longer be confined within the four walls of the school. Education has to be provided in a variety of ways both within the school and outside the formal system with the active involvement of the community.

Effectiveness of the programme can be gauged only in relation to the benefits that have resulted from the learning process. The follow-up is very important both in terms of the learning needs for development and for literacy and continuing education. An aspect that has to be emphasized is the need to link literacy and education with social needs. There is also the need for humility on the part of the teachers and to make education a genuine, two-way learning process. There is much to be learnt from the learners and this has to be conveyed to them to make the group participate more actively. Teaching methods and materials, as far as possible, should be related to the learner's needs and cannot be standardised. Inexpensive local materials need to be utilised.

We have the third largest manpower trained in science and technology in the world. The Ramamurthy Committee on the review of National Policy on Education recognised that education is an investment in terms of human beings and that this asset needs to be strengthened with an element of dynamism. Each individual is important and his dignity and contribution should be fully recognised and appreciated in the new educational system. The emphasis has to be placed on learning rather than on teaching. It should be activity-based, innovative and exploratory.

Curriculum Rationale

The curriculum should be framed taking into account all the aspects of human life. Core curriculum elements including moral and spiritual values, work experience, national integration, etc. must be incorporated in it. Other than being regular in attending classes everyday, one should ensure that pictures, flip charts, models and film strips, etc. are used judiciously so that students' retention capability increases and teaching becomes a more effective and joyful experience. It is difficult to apply a uniform approach to all. The teachers and instructors should have the freedom of evolving a curriculum with the minimum amount of classification and codification. The amount of interaction is determined by day-to-day needs. Curriculum has therefore to be ultimately redrawn and redefined. Whether it is classroom teaching, out of the classroom interaction or non-formal education, the content has absolutely no meaning till it has been linked to a tangible result that can be seen. Core curriculum areas may be common and compulsory for all, but there has to be a built-in flexibility in transaction. The devices used for transaction may differ from one place to another and even from one region to another in a state.

The teaching methodology may be linked to the learning needs of the group. Literacy is to be treated as an input. The dissemination has been purely of a technical nature so far. The need is to classify the information in a manner in which it can be tabulated so that the same could reach the people easily. For instance, in the case of programmes on physical education and health, it is easy to reach out to the vast number of people through village level health workers programme and the curriculum development has to be drawn in consultation with the village level health workers, the community and the specialists.

The role of audio-visual materials in learning also becomes important. because such materials enrich the visual and audio experiences of the learner. It is essential to take up the tasks of building resources to support the curriculum.

India has a rich tradition of art and culture. Indigenous toys and games developed and available in the villages can significantly contribute to the teaching-learning process, organised systematically. One could motivate groups of different kinds of people—scientists, engineers, doctors, etc. in the tasks of making learning joyful and providing innovative experiences. One could perhaps produce several packages of materials. But there is also a need to enrich the experiences of poor children. One has to look closely at the learning situation for every identifiable group of young learners and analyse the situation in terms of learning resources, strategies, processes, practices and outcomes. The outcomes of learning in any situation, whether it is natural, improvised or institutionalised, depend very much on the objectives and how these objectives have been translated and brought into the learning exercise of the child. Any analysis of the learning situation should at least include these aspects. Most often the objectives of learning are not clear, neither to the teacher nor to the learner. In order to make learning purposeful and self-motivating, it is necessary to know what the child is to learn and wants to do and then plan the learning experiences in such a way that there is a matching of his expectations.

The child is curious about living objects around him including man, woman and himself. He soon discovers that there are recurring patterns and stable patterns of human relationships and behaviour. He is curious about animals, society, market, government and so on. There are so many questions to which there is no end. The fact is that the child tries to relate himself to the world around him through his knowledge, activities and feelings.

New methods and procedures may be evolved to encourage participation of school children in various activities related to ecological conservation and preservation. The children may be involved in these activities through a series of cooperative societies and organisations which could be set up in schools and in the centres of continuing education all over the country in a phased manner. The role of these institutions will be to take active part in disseminating the information gained from various sources among the people in their localities. The plan may aim at educating children about their immediate environment and the causes for its deterioration, impart knowledge about the different facets of the eco-system, their interdependence and their need for survival and to mobilise youngsters by instilling in them the spirit of scientific enquiry. Practical knowledge about environmental protection may be imparted through audio-visual aids, posters, quiz programmes, lectures and inexpensive experiments.

Basic Problems

There is a need to evolve a curriculum which is based on the interest of the learners with emphasis on crafts and skills in various occupations. The curriculum formulated at the national level with an urban outlook is not going to solve the problems. In fact, the process of development should be the other way round, i.e. from the village level to block level, district and to state level. One of the basic problems of literacy and continuing education has been the perception of planners that the teacher would carry the programme into the village on the basis of bare skeleton facilities. Most of our teachers in the villages specially those who participate in the programmes have to face environmental problems. They require to use different methods and techniques so that the learners are willing to accept new methodology. The programme of massive orientation of teachers which was initiated in 1986 needs to be continued with variety and necessary changes so that the teachers could get training in new innovations and ideas.

Educational Materials and Aids

Besides development of curriculum, educational materials may be prepared and used in which learners and community are actively involved. Educational materials have so far remained specific and correlated to immediate issues and capable only for limited circulation. Apart from pictures, use of posters, film strips, puppets, *kirtan* groups, *bhajan mandalies* could be very effective in such a situation. The local resources have to be developed and this is something which is lacking in most of our ongoing programmes of literacy and continuing education. Sarpunches and many other field functionaries are to be treated as very strong and important agents in any educational programme. They are to be utilised most effectively for education and learning about new methods and techniques about which the teachers do not have enough information. If these people can be tapped, there will be enough educational resources in the villages to strengthen the educational process. Literacy and continuing education should be completed with the objective establishing classroom links with the community, creating and understanding of the needs of the children and ways of meeting them, help people to acquire relevant knowledge and skills and stimulate individual and group action for better living.

Literacy and continuing educational programmes being carried out fail to sustain the interest of the learners who are mainly engaged in day long labour in the fields and on the roads. The programme reduces the status of the person in the family and in his immediate environment unless these are based on prestige and support that could be mobilised locally. There is a need for the family approach in which an effort could be made to create a responsible structure in the community where learning has greater success in eliciting participation and adoption of new practices. Literacy and continuing educational programmes can make a dent only if they are relevant to the needs of the learners. They should be related to the solution of problems centred around the new world and the examples quoted should be from the area of health, agriculture, environment and the vocations. Formal instruction or bureaucracy cannot tackle this problem. It needs to be supplemented by the efforts of voluntary organisations, community and motivating individuals and groups. Imparting education of any kind is not easy. Even in ordinary formal school education, teaching alphabets is a difficult task. It needs much more analysis while dealing with problems of sociology and economics in the rural areas. It has to deal with marginal farmers, landless labourers and their children and naturally the entire motivational complex is related to this problem. One has to understand what kind of motivation can possibly be utilised so that the literacy programme can succeed.

Perhaps along with the textbooks and teacher's guides, it is very essential to preplan the preparation and utilization of teaching aids by involving the learners and communities so that both participate in the processes actively. At the primary level, in order to keep the interest of the learners, one can propose to prepare programmes based on dramas, games, and other related activities, It is essential to carry on experiments and explore ways and means in the area of literacy and continuing education. For instance, while finalising the scheme, the idea of raising finances for the development of the village can be mooted by suggesting various options which are available in the village so that learners could judge by themselves as to whether the loan from the *Sahukar* or cooperative bank should he taken and which option shall be beneficial for them. Similarly, consequences of taking loans for non-productive purposes would amount to be going into the mouth of snake in a game of Snakes and Ladders, which could be developed for the programme.

If simple graphic teaching aids in the form of models of real things are designed in collaboration with the village artisans, teachers and learners, the difficult concepts in science and mathematics can be easily comprehended. The school system has neither any teaching aids nor the funds to purchase any aids. There is also a question of maintaining the aids for lack of proper storage facilities. The system seldom encourages the use of such aids. Teaching aids in the present situation have a very low priority, though these help to promote learning by actual participation. There is a need to devise ways and means to motivate the preparation of improvised teaching aids and earmark a time slot for their planning and preparation. Learning activities can be planned while considering their necessity and relevance. The learner feels interested only when activities involve identification of difficult concepts. The aids and activities would help to solve the basic problems of drop-outs and adult literacy skills effectively. Permanent tools for lifelong learning and for facing some of the immediate situations in life are areas where literacy is indispensable. Equal emphasis should be laid on both the aspects of the programme, i.e. conscientisation and alphabetisation. There should be ample stress on the training of teachers and they should be taught to make use of the educational materials being provided to them. A training programme for teachers must be initiated at different levels. Since it is difficult to train all the teachers at one central place at the same time, it is suggested that teacher trainers be employed at different levels. Since the role of these teacher trainers is in no way insignificant, it is suggested that they be given a kind of orientation on how to train the teachers and also how to make the best use of the teaching aids. Naturally, the orientation programme should be as informative as possible.

(B) PRODUCTION OF EDUCATIONAL MATERIAL FOR ADULT EDUCATION PROGRAMME – A CASE STUDY

The Government of India launched a massive National Adult Education Programme (NAEP) to reach this target within the next 5-10 years and allocated more than Rs. 200 crores in the Sixth Five-year Plan towards its implementation. Though the Adult Education Programme had been in existence in the country for more than forty years, it was the first time that such gigantic efforts were attempted by the government. It adopted much more open philosophy towards this programme than hitherto followed. Government, semi-government, autonomous as well as voluntary agencies were encouraged to begin literacy classes on a nationwide scale. Similarly, widest possible utilization was being explored with media such as films, TV, radio, sound filmstrips to encourage, involve, motivate the adults of rural and urban areas. during early eighties of the last century.

Since the adults in question came largely from rural areas and because of social, cultural and linguistic differences from one region/state to another, different attempts were made to prepare educational material most suited for the audience. But very often such attempts tend to generate only a primer, sometime a workbook and may be, a teacher's guide. Very rarely has there been an attempt in an integrated way to prepare other AV forms such as charts, flashcards, flannelboard, cut-outs, games, etc. which could generate as well as sustain the interest of adults in the educational process over a long stretch of six to eight months. If there were words, as there have to be in any language teaching what could be these words? If there are visuals in books, charts what kind of visuals or drawings they may be and in what manner were they to be used in the field situation? How could the training to supervisors and teachers be planned? Above all, could there be a systematic and logical way to link the various steps of production of educational material with the problems concerning illiterate adults of area.

About the Work

This describes the work related to the preparation of educational material for the rural adults of Delhi and Haryana State. The work reported here deals with the process, methodology or the system design which emerged during the course of preparation of the material. It is not the intention of the author to suggest that this is the only way to produce the material. The following types of material were produced in this project.

(i) Primer; (ii) Workbook; (iii) Wall Chart; (iv) Mini Flash Cards; (v) Cutouts; (vi) A Game; and (vii) Teachers' Guide

To say that all the different steps had been preplanned would be to negate the very basis of undertaking this project. It would instead be more appropriate to say that the system emerged from the basic approach of not taking anything for granted and to question every assumption on which rested the past experience of literacy programme. Hence, while writing it becomes necessary to trace the process as the work began and how gradually it began to take a definite shape.

The Team and the Venue

The first step was to identify the nature of team which would be involved in this and where would the team work towards the preparation of material. The answers to both were easy. Firstly, the venue of work should not be in Delhi but instead should be in some village away from it, may be in Haryana, Village Khori, whereas the team could also interact with rural environment and adults for whom the material was to be prepared. Delhi could act as a base for follow-up work. Secondly, the team should not only consist of linguists or persons traditionally associated with literacy programme only. If possible, there should be in the team young social workers, whose direct experiences of rural adult could bring in fresh ideas and realism in the educational materials. The team was, therefore, composed of persons with adult literacy background from the Directorate of Adult Education, New Delhi, Literacy House, Lucknow; Linguists from the Department of Social Sciences and Humanities, NCERT; Social Works, Research Centre, Tilnia and Khori; writers and artists, photographers and educational technologists from the Department of Teaching Aids of NCERT. Throughout the course of five months in which neary five workshops were organised, the team remained essentially the same, working at Khori and Delhi.

Basic Assumptions on Adult Education

The notions about adult education amongst the team members were as diverse as their background. One could broadly classify their approach into the following:

(a) **Conscientisation:** Some of the team members were of the view that the basic objective of the programme should only be conscientisation of the adults about their problems, rights and possible ways to solve their plight. The teacher should work on this aspect and along with, teach literacy without any book. Several questions were raised on this approach. Would all the teachers have sympathy and understanding of the rural adults, problem to adopt such an open-minded learning method and yet have the adults reach certain take-off level of literacy skills? The answer was surely, no. Only few teachers may have the insight and commitment.

(b) **Literacy Skills :** One group in the team believed that the adult in question is interested in his own education because he can see the logic of being literate, to being educated, to becoming economically better off. Therefore, the exercise of preparing educational material should be to provide the literacy and numeracy skills only which may be developed on linguistic basis. This viewpoint generated a host of questions from the workers with long experience of literacy classes who had been frustrated with this approach. After a brief initial period of curiosity, the adult classes looked deserted for want of sustained interest and motivation.

(c) **Community Action Based :** There were some team members who put forth the idea that adult education programme should be group and community action based. The idea being that developmental activities would form the common objectives of the adults and the literacy aspects could be woven around it. It was agreed that this would perhaps be an ideal situation, but quite often the developmental inputs requiring coordination between various ministries, is not readily available in rural circumstances. To generate motivation amongst the community members for development work would once again imply a very committed teacher which may be very rare.

(d) Combination of Viewpoints : Was it possible then to take a view that would be combination of all the above three points of views of conscientisation, literacy skills and community action? It was not only essential to generate motivation in learners in the beginning, but more important, to sustain it throughout the entire programme so that the curve of motivation never dips too low to create the problem of heavy dropouts. Hence, the educational material may be developed around the three concepts which may also form the three distinct phases of an adult education class everyday. The initial linguistic difficulties often found amongst adults, might not be problematic provided motivation of the adult to attend the class was strong. This meant the content material to be dominated and linguists should serve this. Was it possible to link conscientisation and alphabetisation? Would putting them together to prepare problem oriented and need based material bring enormous strain on the writers? Would it violate the principles of beginning the literacy skills from the simplest linguistic unit? Would this team be able to identify the typical problems of the rural adults to put them across in the textbook form? Obviously, we had more questions than answers.

Who is Adult ?

The cultural gap being wide as it is between the urban and rural community, there was much to learn about them through SWRC social workers as well as by direct experience. The rural adult between the age of 15-35 years, in this programme can essentially be considered to be a landless poor or at best, a marginal farmer. His day-to-day problems were fundamentally economic—of work, wages, food, clothing, medicine, etc. If at all he was remotely interested in education, it was his child's. It was difficult to perceive any motivation on his part for his own education. He felt he knows simple arithmetic and enough about agriculture to meet the needs of his daily life. The life of his family members existed critically throughout the year on two square meals a day. He wanted to know about agriculture and do his best for his crops or where could he get work and adequate wages to make his meagre ends meet. The older generation (retired head-master, priest, book seller) were highly sceptical about the present educational system which rendered their youth after schooling, incapable of either working on the farm to get any gainful employment. Under such circumstances how is it possible to bring the rural adult within the folds of education, sustain his interest for seven-eight months at a stretch? Are there some aspects which might attract him, motivate him or kindle his interest?

Possible Factors of Motivation in Adults

The team members after several informal sessions with the villagers, arrived at some possible motivational factors in their lives. These could be classified as being :

(a) direct and immediate economic gains;

(b) awareness, understanding of their problems, their causes and possible solutions;

(c) entertainment (folk music, drama festivals, movies, etc.); and

(d) involvement in the activities of the class and the educational process.

Other motivations or interests of the rural adult could be extensions of these or perhaps of some more. Thus, the educational classes would have to discard the formal look prevalent so often but instead adopt a highly informal atmosphere. The literacy element may have to be underplayed at least in the initial few months and carefully woven with informal discussions, entertainment and educational activities related to their environment even at the cost of extending the time period (7-8 months) or reducing the basic learning objectives (vocabulary and operations with numbers). Could such rigidities be dispensed with by the teacher in the field situation and if so, what kind of educational material be prepared which could help in building an informal atmosphere?

Line of Action

The basic approach towards the preparation of material then emerged as:

(a) Identify list of common and crucial problems of the rural adult community after interaction with them;

(b) Weave a story around these problems to provide the topic for informal discussions;

(c) Select key words (simple) to develop lessons (more words, sentences) on them;

(d) Work on visuals for story, lessons through photographs, drawings by artists as well as villagers;

(e) Meet the adults at night again to get their reactions on material prepared; and
(f) Review amongst the team members, the experiences of each day and develop the material further.

Spoken Language

An issue closely linked with the material preparation and motivation of adults, was the use of spoken language as mentioned in the policy statement on adult education. It was argued that if spoken language was to be used, then there cannot possibly be a common primer for the State of Haryana and Delhi. The spoken language often varies from district to district and hence, there could be a core vocabulary on which the primer is based in standard form of spoken Hindi. As regards the concept of core vocabulary prepared on the basis of the frequency counts of words and letters, it was felt that most of such counts were based on the written form of the language. They had been prepared for school books and the needs of various learners' groups—male and female, rural and urban community differ vastly. Hence, it may not be tenable in the present context and we may have to build the vocabulary accord-ing to our needs.

Some More Questions

As the work progressed, questions kept surfacing which were discussed in small groups. At times, local persons were contacted to verify the authenticity of a statement and the meaning of a particular word. Should there be two primers — one each for men and women? Most of the team members were of the view that there should be two but perhaps this could be attempted after one primer for both is put in operation and feedback obtained on it.

Story : Should there be different stories for each lesson or a single theme running throughout the lessons? If a single theme, then what sort of central character could be there who could create sympathy amongst the learners? Obviously, it had to be a marginal farmer who had to work as a labourer on the farms most of the year. The stories centered around him and other characters to resemble the community.

Lessons : What words should come first and how should they be sequenced? Whether the story would suggest the key words or the key words essential for the lesson would become a part of the story? What should be the number of new sound symbols in each lesson? Should the lesson begin with a sentence or just words? Should the words be analysed into graphics, i.e. Ram into Ra-Ma? Or would it be better to introduce words as a whole for full recognition? Should the words be built into sentences? If yes — then at what stage? Can a lesson be divided into parts and can each part function as an independent sub-unit of a lesson? It was agreed that except the first lesson, no lesson should have more than four sound symbols, two in each sub-units and each new key word should have only one new element, e.g. in DAM (price) and DAWA (medicine) only DA and WA are new elements, if MA has been introduced earlier. Attempts should be made as far as possible to choose the sounds on frequency basis provided they occur in the story. Alternative key words used in the lesson should be exploited in the story.

Pictures : What should the pictures relate to story, key words? Should the pictures be taken from real life, through photographs or sketches, or perhaps both? They may be drawn in bold lines with two colour scheme for less expensive printing?

Charts : Would there be a necessity of charts for the teacher? If yes, what kind? If they are to serve the purpose of better communication then what should be the size? After some experimentation, it was felt that the size of flip charts (each page corresponding to a lesson of the primer), may be about 16^0 X 24^0 containing the picture of the story, as in primer. It may also contain the key words on each page. The utility of the charts may be much more in the beginning; so they may be prepared for the first half of the primer only.

Workbook : What all elements should go in the workbook on which the adult is to practise the writing skill? If a letter or word is to be copied, should there be enough indications about the directions of the stroke? Should the workbook also contain reading material and pictures? Yes, some pictures, some reading material but mostly the writing space, the earlier part of which could show the direction of the strokes to help the learners.

Teacher's Guide : Whether teacher's guide ought to be in a separate book form or should the guidelines to teachers be included in the primer itself ? If they are to be provided in the primer then where? Would it make the primer much too bulky? It was suggested that there are to be two types of information to be given to the teacher—one dealing with philosophy, methodology, approach and how the material was prepared; the second information may be linguistic or dealing with literacy skills. The first one could be given separately in a booklet and the second one as footnotes in the primer.

Other Materials : What could be other material which would motivate discussion and activities in the adult education class. The cutouts of village life and scenario could be used on a flannel board made out of a gunny bag or jute cloth to tell a story. The story or incident could be narrated by the learners or teachers. The activities could revolve around the talent available in and around the village as well as the material — natural and waste for the preparation of simple teaching aids. Could one also develop a game based around the economics of rural adult?

The first phase of educational material had begun to take place. Several days of work at Khori was followed by two separate sessions at Delhi. The work on material started at Khori was developed further so that it could be tested or assessed once again with the adults at Khori.

Pretesting the First Stage

The second visit of the team to Khori was made with two objectives —(i) to pretest some of the ideas and materials—stories, words, sentences, pictures, game and overall methodology and (ii) to revise and develop the material further. About 30-35 rural illiterate adults were brought every night for a week to attend group and class sessions. In groups of five or six adults feedback was taken on stories, pictures and art work. The problem oriented themes evoked animated discussion. The class sessions involved all the adults put together to react on the teaching by one of the team members while others watched. Reactions were also recorded when the class was conducted by some rural youth who had earlier been involved in the work.

Observations made during the night sessions were critically analysed during the day and further work was done in groups by the team members. Some of the analysis went as follows:

Stories : The stories were interesting but tended to be very serious? Was there a necessity to bring some humour in them? Questions were also raised if the stories were urbanised viewpoint on rural setting?

Primer : While completing the work on the primer, the size and format came under constant discussion. There was genuine difficulty in keeping all the norms of the literacy skills with our approach and yet keep it around 100 pages. It was felt that it was not the bold letters which were important but the clarity and spacing between them.

Numbers : The session with rural adults on numbers was perhaps most revealing. The adult is familiar with operations such as addition, subtraction, multiplication and division. In fact, some of them were able to calculate the interest in one year on Rs. 275/- at the rate of two percent per month faster than the team members. However, he may not be able recognise or write the cardinal numbers. What would be best manner to achieve this literacy skill? Since the adult is familiar and recognised the currency notes and coins by size and shape, it was agreed that the symbol of coins be used in the primer and workbook for making the adult recognize the numbers. The primer would also contain the various arithmetic operations, counting up to 1,000 and the units of length, area, volume, weight and time.

Alphabets and Words : In try-out exercise, the very passive teaching session was totally transformed with minicards having alphabets and words. Adults became lively and responsive in the identification of alphabets and joining some to make new, their own words. Minicards made out of used match boxes opened up new possibilities of teaching and involving the adults in the learning process.

Game : The idea of a game arose in our minds when we saw the adults in Khori huddled together and playing a game similar to Ludo with dice and moving their different shaped pieces along squares arranged in design on cloth. We designed one similar to Trade or Monopoly which makes the adults read the numbers and do some arithmetic operations. In addition, it was to be related to their rural environment—the market, bank and the money lender. It also helps them to realise the importance of various options in their lives.

No Machine Operated Devices

No machine operated device (film video slides, filmstrip, overhead transparencies, audiotape, etc.) were planned. It was felt that the use of hardware and its maintenance in rural conditions would not be a practical proposition. Furthermore, the high cost of machines and lack of proper software (programmes) would make the devices uneconomical.

Final Products

All the material to be used in the field situation has to be only in the printed form and based on the necessities of an average rural teacher. It may evoke response from adults and the teacher to create their own materials. The basic form of educational material emerging from this project consisted the following seven items.

Primer (About 100 pages, 38 Lessons): It has hints for teacher; the stories for him to read to the adults; the lessons on alphabets and numeracy; pictures related to stories and key words. The stories deal with questions on wages, food, medicine, disease, nutrition, agriculture and marketing, etc.

Workbook (About 100 pages): It has hints for teachers on how to use the workbook. The lessons on practising the writing skill is related to the lessons of the primer. There are sums in arithmetic finally ending with the exercise of filling up forms of post office deposit or sending money.

Charts (For the first 16 lessons of Primer): It has key words and large-sized pictures related to story as in the Primer. The purpose of the charts is to establish communication with the adults.

Cutouts : About 120 drawings of people, places, animals and objects in the rural setting. The cutouts with sandpaper stuck at back are to be used on a gunny bag slipped tightly over a rectangular wooden frame. The cutouts help the adults to tell their own stories related to the story of the primer. It may even motivate the adults to prepare his own visuals and cutouts.

Miniflash Cards (100): For the beginning lessons, minicards of size 2" X 3" were made on which alphabets or words are written. They are meant to be used by adults individually and for them to prepare some more of their own.

Game : The game was printed on a board with a dice and different colour tablets. It consisted artificial currency, bonus cards and a brochure on how to play the game.

Teacher's Guide : It tells the teacher about the methodology of preparation of educational material; how to make best use of the various items and the possibilities of various activities to be carried out with the adults to involve them in the learning process. It also tells them what all they may have to do in order to gain their confidence.

The Adult Class

It was felt that the field situation where Adult Education Programme would operate, cannot exist merely on the basis of literacy. From the basic assumptions on AEP made earlier, it would be logical to conceive the place as a community centre where adults—men and women— may gather at night.

Three-four segments of the educational class would consist of:

(a) The conscientisation process (first 30 minutes): It would consist of discussing the story of the Primer, drawing parallel examples out of the real life and start discussion on questions given and many more that may be raised. The narration of problems of the adults from their own experiences could be done by using cutouts. If the teacher is adventurous it could even be staged and the adults could act and role play the situation.

(b) Language and Numeracy Skills (40 minutes): The next half hour or more could be spent in imparting the literacy skills through primer, workbook, flash cards charts, etc.

(c) Activities: The last segment of the evening programme would consist of either organising (i) some cultural event such as keertan, puppet show, theatre, etc. or (ii) lecture, demonstration of some person working in agriculture, handicraft, business, medicine, banking etc. speaking to adults on a topic of direct interest to them (iii) adults working individually or to prepare educational material from their own resources and environment, they could revise the game, chart, flash cards to suit their own dialect or they could after a few months, prepare wall news paper and items such as sun dial to know time, signs or name plates on the road. They could prepare a wall diagram on local weather report, prices of grain market, display some official letter as to how it is to be written. An ideal situation would be when a teacher with the help of the adult learners could bring out their own primer or workbook and other supplementary materials.

(d) Teacher's Planning : Of course, the most vital element of day-to-day programme would be the every day planning required on the part of the teacher. What problems of the adult demand information or help? Where can we get them? Whom should he contact? What kind of activities are envisaged and how to entrust responsibilities to the learners? And how can he do all these without major interruption in adult education session in the evening? A tall order for a part-time teacher.

Administration and Teachers' Training

While the production of educational material is related to the needs of the target audience and the learning objectives to be achieved, the team members time and again, began to see the linkage with teacher obviously and the district or state administration developmental inputs, etc. All are interrelated with each other. If the exercise is concerned with a primer, literacy skills, attendance of adults (true or false) then the consequence cannot be significantly different from the experience of the past forty years—that of heavy dropouts and relapse into illiteracy after a year or so. If not, then the authorities would have to seek new ways of administering these projects.

The key person in the programme would be the teacher. It would be his empathy, dedication, interest and innovation on which will depend the success of the programme. Even if some of these qualities were there in this person, he would need training. But not of the formal kind of which the trainers and he himself are a product of—rigidity of rules, attendance, timings, curriculum, achievement level, etc. One would have to unlearn many of these aspects to create enormous flexibility into the educational process in which the adult begins to see relationship between his problems and getting literate. Hence, the training of teacher has to consist of knowing the problems of the community, knowing where help and information can be sought for and having the resourcefulness to coordinate between various agencies. The teacher surely cannot do all this alone but the training could help the teachers in that block or district. The training of teachers would require him and the local administration to identify crafts, raw materials, processes and marketing system to build confidence amongst the adults. In short, his training must not be of formal nature because the field situation is going to demand from him (and administration) non-formal practice in an informal style. The method to monitor and evaluate such programme has to be done in a different way. How can incentives be given to the field workers? One way can be to encourage the teacher to produce educational material which can be the criteria to evaluate the success of the class and on which awards can be given to villages and the teacher. The AEP, in other words, though financed at the state level can have an opportunity to grow from the grassroots level.

□

7

(A) MEDIA SUPPORT FOR CURRICULUM TRANSACTION

Teaching methods and materials cannot be standardised and have to be related to the learner's environment. Inexpensive local material and technology need to be used to strengthen the educational processes. The teachers can involve the children in creative drama situations to facilitate the teaching of languages and environmental sciences. Similarly in mathematics, the children dissemble and assemble parts of a model, explore and discover the intricacies of its morphology and topology and get motivation through the thrills of work and play and simultaneously comprehend the concepts with ease. Playway methods, acting, singing are some of the activities essential for making learning concrete, effective and joyful as these are closely related to the life both inside and outside the school environment and encourage children to raise questions, to probe, explore and record their own observations. These activities enable them to develop a sense of confidence and make useful contributions to the society.

With the advent of educational technology which implies a systematic way of designing and implementing the process of teaching and learning, based on research of the human nature and employing all resources, both human and non-human to achieve the objective, it is possible to promote universalisation of education. New methods and materials are being evolved at the formal and non-formal levels of education. The textbook still remains the sole instructional material in India. Its availability and adequate use has always been doubtful. Perhaps one of the main reasons why we could not make headway in achieving universalisation of elementary education so far, is that we provide the text books, teachers' guides and workbooks without any reflection and inputs of the media which are essential as reinforcements to enrich the experiences of the learners.

Integration of Elements of the Media

In an era of communication with the growing explosion of educational media, it is possible to supplement the textbook-oriented process of learning. It could be a pictorial package, set of charts, improvised puppets or the instructional television programme.

A pictorial package consisting of 15-20 large size sheets comprising photographs, and illustrations of an idea, concept or a situation from the curriculum for a subject or a particular concept, logically analysed into various steps or stages, could be integrated with the text. These packages may serve as multipurpose devices for group teaching. Some of these can be displayed in the classroom to serve as a stimulus for motivation, revision and reinforcement.

Study kits or multi-media packages consisting of graphic aids, models, slides, folders pertaining to specific concepts or themes may be designed and selected to elaborate the subject. These materials can be kept in the built-in boxes. Study kits and science kits were improvised by the NCERT in the past and supplied to the schools. The kits provide the basic reading observation skills for preparing a solid background of information. They involved the learners and motivated them to go deep into a subject by related references. Study kits provide a rich variety of teaching tools and curriculum materials to the teachers and students for improving their teaching-learning techniques and for creating a better intellectual environment in the schools.

Improvised and creative puppets have enormous possibilities in the development of purposeful activities in the classroom. These puppets can be made to suit various teaching-learning situations. Hand puppets, rod puppets and string puppets from a variety of material can be developed to depict different characters or situations. The materials are paper, cardboard, tree branches, coconuts, ribbon, balls, wire, wood, buttons, pins, rubbers etc. Even scrap and inexpensive material can be utilised for making puppets. A set of stock puppets can be developed and used for developing a story depending upon the puppet characters, animals, etc. It is necessary to develop a creative drama situation through role playing situations to provide the verbal content.

Playing is a natural way of child's exploration by developing senses, awareness of beauty, utilisation of puppetry and creative drama as a co-curricular activity which should be encouraged in the elementary schools so that the teachers with their skills, guide the children into the creative drama situations in languages and environmental studies.

Improvised Teaching Aids

Self-made teaching aids have manifold advantages over those which are commercially produced or mass produced. The pre-requesities of these aids are the basic preparedness, quality of the subject matter, proper planning, inherent factors for effective teaching, material available in the immediate environment and fabrication of teaching aids with the involvement of teachers, children and the community. The content of such an aid shall adequately fit into the teaching unit. It would be inexpensive and suited to the local needs and conditions. Even if a specific concept takes a longer time to teach, if taught with the help of self-made aids, the ultimate gains in the form of permanent and functional learning will be much more and the overall teaching time in a class will be considerably reduced. Since the teachers are part of the preparation process of such aids, they are likely to use them in the classroom situations with confidence. Manuals of teaching aids have been devised for difficult concepts with write-ups and illustrations so that the teachers, with involvement of the community can prepare aids from the locally available materials.

These efforts enable the teachers to develop a culture of educational media with specific reference to the content of the subject matter. They can establish relationships by linking the principles with the methods and materials which could be commonly used in the various branches of mathematics and science. The manuals aim at getting the students actively involved in the concepts through the processes of preparation of models and other teaching aids into perceptual experiences. The teaching-learning aids are materials which help the learner to grasp the subject taught and comprehend without much efforts. The learning materials that have been native to science and laboratories could come into existence in their natural course to facilitate learning.

The situation of mathematics learning has become so critical that aids have necessarily to be innovated and concreteness restored which has become so abstract that the young learners are getting scared of the subject. When the learner dissembles and assembles part of a model, explores and discovers the intricacies of its morphology and topology, he/she will be able to create one like it which may not be quite similar. The thrills of work and play with it is related emotionally in every respect. A combination of models of maths, in a form of mathematics kit can serve as a torch-bearer to the learners for better comprehension of the concepts with ease.

The contingency funds provided to each school are quite meagre and completion of the syllabus is the main worry of the teachers. In such situations, the manuals may be developed on some selected teaching aids providing concise textual information with regard to the availability of materials in the environment, selection of different concepts, the media, format selection of preparing the aids with the available material and the involvement of the community in the preparation process. Once the teachers/parents implement the strategies outlined in the manuals, children can find themselves discovering the intricacies of the concepts on their own and that will develop in them a life-long aptitude for the concerned subject matter. The presentation and treatment of topics provide a rich source of ideas, be it in mathematics or science for the science/maths clubs or fairs which can become the hallmark of progressive schools. Basic concepts, if concretised through the models would enrich the experiences of the students for profound creative thought. At the primary level before each aid is introduced in the class, some sort of activity is needed. This could be in the form of cutting of a strip of paper, collection of seeds or beads or grouping of children. It is necessary to explain the concept and as a reinforcement the aid may be used with illustrations and examples.

Imparting training to children in the acquisition of skills through interactive and repetitive exercises continues to be considered respectable since it carries the backing of tradition. In nursery and even in primary schools, the children are encouraged in this practice especially in mathematics though it runs counter to nature with the result that it kills the initiative of logical thinking and insight of the child. Research findings in many countries bear ample testimony to the need for adoption of strategies which provide children appropriate and adequate experiences for abstracting ideas and finding their ways to get at concepts with long-term benefits characterised by learning through self-confidence and initiative. A concept or a sub-concept should find a place in the syllabus only after it is established that it has the potentials of concretisation. If the teachers substitute verbalism and symbolism under the plea of promoting sheltered learning to pass the examination, the child finds itself blocked and strait-jacketed as it kills the initiative and exploration instinct which is otherwise inherent in every child. The child is bewildered to find himself in a fix and struggles to climb up the ladder of reality. He tries to encounter and reconciles himself but is ultimately disappointed. Most of the teachers do not prepare and use the teaching-learning aids on the plea that such an exercise is time consuming and it is no possible to under take this work due to the prevailing conditions in the schools as their major concern is to complete the syllabus. If high standards of learning are to be ushered in and better concretisation is to be ensured, the objectives can be achieved through special programmes of mass media which could bring fundamental changes in the pupil-teacher relationships. Model examples of the improvised teaching aids are listed in the chapter on Technological Aids.

Audio-Visual Aids

The content of communication involves complex ideas and concepts. Mere words are artificial and do not develop images in the minds of the readers and listeners easily. Pictures are nearer to perception than verbal abstractions. As far as possible ideas need to be concretised and converged in pictorial images. Educational materials can be made more clearer and expressive if the ideas can be turned into pictures by simple sketches merely through the outlines of objects and processes. Little artistic skill is required and one can acquire such skill through practice. Simple sketches can be drawn by the teachers on the chalkboard in a teaching learning situation. The verbal-cum-pictorial language in pictures is more expressive than through the spoken or written word. Even basic symbols of communication can serve as the most useful and effective teaching-learning tools dovetailed into the text material.

Researches during the last few decades have proved that teaching through the television to supplement the curriculum is more effective. Under the present appalling figures of illiteracy the total system of a variety of media and particularly educational television have to be built into the development of instructional materials to revitalise and enrich the educational practices. Educational TV provides one of the most dynamic, modern and potential inputs in the curriculum to achieve the desired standards. ETV and the textbooks are both complementary to one another. In order to generalise the TV presentations and to optimise their use we have to cut across the existing syllabi in different states.

Certain core concepts and concepts of the curriculum can be culled out to be weaved into the television telecasts by providing a scope for all India coverage. TV can prove to be a vital and effective instruments when programmes about national integration, freedom movement, value education, Yoga, etc. are telecast systematically all over the country which has now been made possible through the satellite communication network.

Great emphasis is required to be placed on the projection of teacher education programmes through the TV so that improvements and innovations could provide a structure which will percolate down to the grass-roots, viz. the classrooms. ETV programmes for teachers could help in broadening the horizons of knowledge, awareness and understanding. For the development of functional literacy, television programmes can do wonders and tackle the problem of the vast number of illiterates in the country. Simple and inexpensive media can be utilised to suffuse the visual perception of the viewers. Such media are easily available through the rich cultural heritage, traditions and practices. There are correlated visuals such as flash cards, filmstrips and flannel graph packages.

TV is the best media for explaining the concepts involving motion such as working engine, electric circuits, etc. Similarly, the number of science concepts and experiments can be best projected through television for concretisation. Translating syllabi into possible television uses, identifying topics where television can be most effective, stating behavioural objectives for the identified units and key concepts are part of the ETV programme planning. Preparation of models for the scripts to fit into the local situations is a mental exer-cise for producing the television programmes. Before undertaking the programmes in a series mode, it is essential to test the prototype with the target audience at the script stage. TV has several advantages over the traditional graphic media. It is a cost effective media. With the available transmission slot, a TV programme with a total production cost of ₹10,000 can be viewed by millions at a time. The programme can be made use of through non-broadcasting mode also and to provide reinforcements can be telecast frequently whenever required.

Radio is a rich resource for educational processes at all levels and provides tremendous opportunities for meaningful, effective and widely applicable inputs in the learning process. The All India Radio (AIR) venture in the field of school broadcasts started in 1938 when the Bombay

Station was asked to prepare school programme schedules in collaboration with the State educational authorities. The Government of India has provided more than two lakh and thirty thousand radio-cum-cassette players to schools under the Educational Technology scheme to have an access to the educational broadcast in India. The broadcasts cover subjects such as Hindi and regional languages from the various stations of All India Radio. The emphasis of the school broadcasts is on curriculum topics developed classwise. Besides, there are a variety of enrichment and teacher training programmes. These broadcasts may be suitably integrated with the curriculum transacted in the schools.

Instructional Programmes

Instructional programmes on television, films or radio are meant for direct classroom teaching, covering definite areas of the curriculum. They elucidate some concept and elaborate the text. Such programmes not only supplement but supplant by providing information and experiences to develop enrichment and background ideas for the basic concepts or the text of the curriculum. The TV has unequivocally acquired a dynamic and dominant role in the entire range of media of communication. TV programmes are generally viewed with physical relaxation, mental receptivity and emotional involvement rather than the dull receptivity and rigidity of the mental discipline that at times accompany the message through the printed media. Television or the motion media has been accepted as the most modern tool of education opening new vistas of adventure in the teaching-learning process. TV not only serves as a powerful medium of entertainment but also as a novel motivational device for changing attitudes, reflecting national aspirations, goals and achievements. For informal out-of-school education, we need information and motivating situations which many times are not reflected in the curriculum. TV programmes serve as an effective medium of mass communication and education by covering such areas which are outside the purview of the school syllabi. A television programme may have the dynamic elements of humour and entertainment interspersed with information to develop definite understanding rather than the dull illustrated lecture pattern.

Joyful Learning

We have first of all to ensure that all the boys and girls at the young age of six years have easy access to joyful teaching-learning methods which can be best provided with media support to the curriculum. This would provide great relief to the learners from the mandatory and rigid curriculum percolating from the Centre to the States, the districts and down to the villages. Things should be the other way round. The concept should be supported with the day-to-day environmental conditioning of the child in his/her immediate school environment so that the learning becomes not only productive but also great fun. Play-way methods, acting, singing are some of the activities essential for making learning effective, joyful and everlasting in the children's minds. Children are fascinated with such activities as they are closely related to their lives both inside and outside the school environment and help them to raise questions, to explore, probe and record their own observations, enabling them to develop a sense of confidence and make useful contributions to the society.

When we say that the curriculum framework needs a relook, we essentially mean the innovative methods, materials and schemes such as Programme of Massive Orientation of School Teachers launched during 1986-89, Minimum Levels of Learning, Operation Block, District Primary Education Project, injected into the curriculum to motivate teachers and learners by providing enriching experiences through the audio-visual media. The National Policy on Education, 1986 and the Programme of Action, 1992 have extensively laid emphasis on the utilisation of media and technology. The influence of the media on the teachers and the taught has a direct bearing on the learning outcomes through positive and responsive behaviour patterns of the society as a whole. Lok Jumbish Parishad, a non-governmental organisation in Jaipur has produced a set of fine ETV programmes on Minumum Levels of Learning in collaboration with Prof. R.H. Dave. These programmes have adequately highlighted the salient factors of the recent explosion of knowledge. The children in the rural and semi-rural areas have easy access to the educational programmes through radio and TV while more sophisticated media like micro processing, computer-aided instructions and Internet, etc. are available with the urban audience. The latter are broad based and cannot come within the purview of the prescribed curriculum. The capability of learning to know would help the learners to acquire the basic skills of numeracy and the process of thinking in day-to-day situations.

Children learn fast when they are involved in some activity, viz. the principle of 'Learning by Doing'. The involvement of the community teaches the children to live together harmoniously. The learning provides the base for the overall development of the child's personality and after the end of primary school, the child should have acquired the skill of communication, confidence, values in life and should be able to appreciate imagination or creative power. All the four pillars of learning can best be achieved with media support.

During practice teaching in the teacher training institutes, the pupil teachers are supposed to prepare a set of charts, models and other teaching aids as part of their assignments, but this remains in theory only and is hardly practised. These aids are got made but not actually prepared by the pupil teachers. In order to ensure that the pupil teachers actually prepare the aids, the practice teaching sessions have to be given more importance.

Training can be imparted to a maximum of 50 teachers in the traditional way but through teleconferencing interactive mode we can cover up to 2,000 persons at a time and reduce the time gap to provide orientation to the teachers. Use of computer-aided instructions at the teacher training level is nearer to reality now. One has to ensure that the idea does not remain on paper but takes practical shape.

(B) OPEN SCHOOLING/COMMON SCHOOLING AND THE ROLE OF THE COMMUNITY

Verdict of the Supreme Court of India regarding admission to the public schools for fulfilling the obligation to provide required amount of freeship to the students belonging to the economically weaker sections of the society is indeed an important and historic step to transform the system of education. This is in conformity with the agreement with the land allotment agencies and would surely aim to promote social integration, accelerate economic growth, moral, social and spiritual values.

Mahatma Gandhi's Talisman often quoted in the textbooks, brought out by the National Council of Educational Research and Training is reproduced in this context. "recall the face of the poorest and the weakest man whom you have seen and ask yourself the step you contemplate is going to be of any use to him. Will he gain anything by it? Will it restore him to a control over his own life and destiny?" When the by-laws were framed by the societies at the time of registration for running the schools and for the allotment of land, it appears that they would meet all the objectives enshrined in Gandhiji's Talisman. It is in the context of the credo that the public schools should view the verdict of Supreme Court of India for implementation in the right earnest. National Policy of Education (1986) described education as a powerful instrument of socio-economic and cultural development, based upon the principles of justice, equality, liberty and dignity of the individuals which help to provide adequate and equal opportunity to every child for developing his personality. The objective of education is on the inculcation of moral, social values and the integration of the rich and the poor children which would surely help in attaining this objective. Unhealthy trend of commercialization of education and the mushroom growth of the private institutions for the privileged few, has done grave damage to the fabric of education in the country.

Meanwhile the affected educational institutions seem to be working out the strategies to overcome the serious crisis and surely be busy in finding out the ways and means which otherwise is liable to adversely affect their earnings if the Supreme Court verdict is implemented in letter and spirit. Some of the public schools have initiated steps of educating the children from the economically weaker sections of the society exclusively in the afternoon, beyond the normal school functioning, hours. This is clearly segregation of the children from the rich and poor sections of the society and would defeat the very purpose for which the verdict has been given by the Supreme Court. As opposed to the Concept Opening Schooling aims at providing educational opportunities to all the children irrespective of the socio-economic considertions of the target audience based upon the principle of equality and social justice. It is also likely that the public schools may start functioning in two shifts, viz. one for the advantaged and affluent group of children and the other shift exclusively for the children from the weaker sections of the society. The schools may also resort to other means and practices. Such methods could be in the form of increased rates for school uniforms, refreshment and snack charges in the canteens, enhancement of payments for the preparation of indentity cards, supervision cards and transport without raising the fee. This may also include the provision of text-books of private publishers other than the books by the NCERT and State textbook bureau which would enable them to pocket huge money in the form of discount, without major economic burden on the parents as these books are not only very costly but often overloaded in the cities and big towns had so far been enjoying the benefit of monopoly and applying restrictions over the admission standards of the educational institutions being run by the government but in the smaller towns and village schools this problem of admission is not so serious. As such there is a great need to monitor the academic and financial aspects of both the private and government institutions, based in the cities and big towns so that there is no disparity and segregation of children from the rich and the poor sections of society as special efforts in providing some relief to good schools is necessary. Public schools have been given land at a very nominal cost and it should be possible to provide subsidy for uniforms, exemption from the payment of tuition fee and other facilities without any charge from the economically and socially weaker sections of the society.

Owing to various socio-economic considerations which bring into focus the process, quality, quantity and other physical constraints, it is essential to tackle these massive problems with utmost urgency and the integrated education of the poor children with the children from the affluent families is one of the steps which are required to be taken to this direction. This should not be restricted to the urban areas but also cover the rural population so that the disparities are reduced and determined measures are initiated to diversification so that the goals of the secularism and socialism are attained through this process of democratic and dynamic innovations. This is in conformity with the commitment to human values and social justice providing equal opportunity to all. It will also aim to remove prejudices and complexities through the unhealthy soeio-economic environment by providing good and quality education irrespective of their capacity to pay.

If the Education Departments in the Centre and the States are vigilant and constantly monitor not only the admission policy of the public schools but also ensure proper academic, physical, socio-economic environment and accounting systems, we can hope for the transition and provision of equality of opportunities to the less-advantaged sections of the society. It is, therefore, meaningful only if the directive of the highest court of judiciary is implemented by the Education Departments with strong determination and vigorous action.

Although statements have been made earlier by the various educationists, political thinkers and social activists to bring quality of access to educational opportunities to all sections throughout the country, providing the principles of social relevance, quality and functional effectiveness of various aspects of education, but such ideas and thoughts have mainly been on paper and it is for the first time in the history of education in India that it is being seriously given due consideration for its implementation when there would be hardly any fundamental difference between the schools run by the government and the private agyncies. All the children shall study and interact with each other in the same environment. Now it has the legal support and it may not be possible to sideline this progressive measure.

The Role of Community Education in Open Schooling

National Policy on Education 1986 described education as a powerful instrument of national development to accelerate the transformation of the social system based upon the principle of justice equality, liberty and dignity of the individual. It aims to provide adequate and equal opportunity to everyone to develop personality to its fullest which to a larger extent is the responsibility of the community. It is envisaged to provide the facilities of education to the children who cannot attend the schools on a regular or on full time basis. Expansion and improvement of education in the developing and under developed areas where there are no schools, is mainly the responsibility of the community at the local level. The concept of part time and own time education needs to be developed on a large scale by the community at every stage so that the facilities may smoothen the transition from school to work and provide opportunities to the large number who are desirous to get educated. Those who had never been to any school can be benefited through participating in the literacy programmes planned by the community from time to time. High priority areas can be covered through rich and varied programmes related to co-curricular activities for the learners. Games and supports may be developed on a large scale in order to improve the physical fitness and sportsmanship with emphasis on the provision of play fields to develop sports which would enhance the process of acquiring literacy.

The formal school system cannot function in isolation. If the child is not attending the school, he has to be in an environment which could be well compared to the school in the form of a non-formal centre. There is already a consciousness to involve voluntary agencies and the community as part of educational priorities so that the base of pyramid of learning becomes strong. Community and parental involvement, vision and learning environment are some of the important aspects which can make or mark the process of learning.

The key to quality education system lies not in adequate funding, but in fruitful utilization by material management techniques which can best be made available through the local community and voluntary organizations. These agencies can play the role to reinforce the natural and integrated character of education. Such bodies are ideally suited to study and examine the educational requirements of the learners in their respective areas of jurisdiction. The major challenge is to provide suitable education for the entire population through involving non-formal community-based educational approaches. These approaches are based to consolidate educational services provided by the community for the non-formal, out of school and drop outs.

Incentives

There are new and emerging areas in literacy which can be taken up by the community. It is important to impart education to around 45 million children who are out of school so as to make them literate and productive. If a child going to school can be given three kilogram rice/wheat per month as an inceptive why such a programme cannot be extended to out-of-school children? The role of the community and non-government organizations (NGOs) to take up the gigantic task of providing meals to the out of school children in open schooling system needs to be stressed. The community and the NGOs at the local level can also assume the responsibility of procurement and service of the meals to such children. The government can transfer the funds to the village Panchayats/ Municipalities and NGOs and simply ensure smooth functioning of programme through periodic regular monitoring, inspections and audits. It would make a significant impact on the achievement of universalisaton of elementary education.

The development of prototype study materials may be taken up by the apex body like National Institute of Open Schooling and disseminated through the regional/state agencies. This needs to be taken up on a priority basis so that it spreads like a movement to bridge the wide gap of achieving universalisation of elementary education. Presently, National Institute of Open Schooling through its accredited institutions/agencies has been catering to nine lakh students while 45 million children are out of school. Enrolment of children for open schooling is a gigantic task to be achieved through the voluntary agencies, NGOs and the community. Multi-thronged strategies like free ration as in the case of children in formal schooling, initiatives of the community and NGOs quality-based study material, application and use of modern communication and information technology such as production and use of audio video programmes computers and teleconferencing—one-way video and two-way audio, are some of the incentives which could be provided to the learners with varying contents. NGOs may play a leadership in the production and dissemination of study materials, equipment to the learners through its accredited centres and the community cooperation can be sought to ensure the optimum benefits. Emphasis should be laid on the measure such as large-scale development of part time and own time education, use of mass media and modern techniques in the teaching learning process in order to make up for the shortcomings in material resources. It is stressed that the right of the parent to decide the kind of education his/her child would receive, is sacrosanct under Article 26(5) of the Constitution. Schemes taken up with the initiative of the Community are doing a pioneering job. Some of these are Mahila Samakhaya (M.P.), Shiksha Karmi National Literary Mission (New Delhi), Social Work and Research Centre, Tilonia (Rajasthan) Eklavya, Bhopal (M.P.), Mitraniketan, Thiruvantapuram (Kerala), etc. These voluntary agencies and NGOs with their dedicated team of education workers have shown excellent results in bringing qualitative as well as quantitative improvements through non-formal system of education. There is a need to choose dedicated and committed persons from the community who could serve as instructors so that the quality of education in open schooling is comparable with the formal school education. This can be possible if learning material of high quality is developed and provided to the learners free of charge. Such centres shall provide participatory learning environment and activities at the local level. Running of these centres will be the responsibility of panchayati raj institutions and voluntary organizations. This is a vital sector to cater to the needs of non-formal learners. For efficient services, there is a requirement for adequate and timely funds. There is a paramount need to create a consciousness of the environment by giving prominence to people's involvement including associations of non-governmental agencies and voluntary efforts. Local community through appropriate bodies may be assigned a major role in various programmes of educational improvement.

Integrated Issues

Many other areas to be covered alongwith education are inter-linking cleanliness, health, cultural identity, national integration, advocating values and creating new impetus for growth and happiness. It is a matter of common experience that the elders in the rural areas, constituting the panchayat Sarpanch would normally promise positive action relating to growth, welfare and education of the children and put their stamp of approval for any new experiments, innovation to demonstrate their willingness for this social cause. The steps envisaged by enthusiastic devoted and committed community workers to educate the local population involve tapping the human and non-human resources and activities for the various age groups and working out strategies at various levels by maintaining a close liaison with the official and voluntary agencies so that the needs of the individual learner and sources of motivation for learning are met through interaction between the learner and the community.

The Open Basic Education programme which offers courses at two levels, viz. A level upto Class III and **B'** level upto class V should be organised jointly by the Open Basic Education Accredited Agencies and the panchayats/municipalities.

Community and Resources

Care is to be taken to see that the study material developed for Open Basic Programme is related to the environment of the learners and they have an easy access. This material could be mainly in the form of games, puppets, charts, cut-outs, models, etc., which may bring in creativity and the children learn subtly and enhance the process of learning.

The activities involving learner imagination can be taken up at the Study Centres in the form of literacy sessions by the community. Such activities can be tried out by the learners at home. Children generally like to renact a story and would be happy if the idea, game or related techniques are demonstrated. Games can be devised in which the clues given are animals, birds and the contestants have to guess what they have in common, i.e., four legs, teeth, etc. Similarly, for getting a loan for ceremonies like marriage or for buying bullocks, which one is productive. There are many options available to procure the loan-bank, mandi or money-lender and which option is the best. Games like 'Snake and Ladder' can be developed, demonstrating these options, and the learners in spare time could play these games and at the same time learn the skill of arithmetic creatively. These devices are, no doubt, less retentative but are generally more imaginative. The learners have the basic advantage of acquiring the skills from the community as they are quite familiar with them and would not hesitate to interact with them. Moreover, the community is well aware of the needs of learners, the community knows what content would be interesting for the children rather than thrusting something which the learners are not ready to accept as the word 'school' is both physical as well as mental torture to the innocent young children. It is important to stimulate interest for knowldege and not to thrust something into their throats so that the children are not denied their right to rest and play besides acquiring knowledge and to learn about the world around him. Community and the NGOs can plan the learning packages rather than learning in conventional model and promote learning based on discussion, interaction and effective use of resources. These agencies can play a consultative role and help to make learning more relevant, based upon discussion of ideas, new approaches and through provision of the best possible materials.

Artisans, such as potters, blacksmiths, carpenters and other related skilled persons are part and parcel of the community in the rural and semi-urban areas who in collaboration with the education workers and NGOs can play a major role in educating the children in Open Schooling System. While the educational workers engaged in imparting literacy in their respective areas can give useful ideas, the artisans are in a position to translate these ideas into viable technological aids and other instructional materials to make learning effective and realistic in sustaining the interests of the learners. The children of the artisans in their places are also in the process of learning through mutual interaction and this indirectly would help in removing the social and caste barriers, which are otherwise very strong in the remote areas of the country.

As on 2nd August, 2017 (H. Times), there are nearly 1.5 million schools across all levels in India. The main purpose of common schooling is that the resources from where they are in excess to where they are needed once to be re-looked at the expansion of schooling facilities made in the previous years and call for a nationwide consolidation of resources in the best interest of the children, avoiding wastage and stagnation. This will provide a better teaching-learning environment and at the same time also make the schools 'Right-to-Education Compliant', leading to the integration of schools with modern technologies. It would be possible to focus at schools than just input-based model, which has been prevailing for decades.

The support of media for the curriculum development in a formal as well as non-formal/open schooling has wider implications but the nature and quantum would differ significantly in each case. While in open schooling situations, the learners are at a distance and scattered, whereas, in the case of formal schooling system, multimedia and inter-activity, through audio-visual media would be more effective. There are core curricular areas in which media does not only supplement the textual materials but also support them.

□

8

NATIONAL POLICIES ON EDUCATION SINCE 1911 WITH SPECIAL REFERENCE TO SCHOOL EDUCATION

National Policies on Education in the form of various resolutions by the Commissions and Committees on Education, constituted over a period of time, have resulted in the transformation of education to meet the needs and aspirations of the people of our country.

TILL 1835, the British rulers did not interfere with the indigenous system of education which laid emphasis on culture rather than on literacy. Two important Resolutions on Indian Educational Policy were published in 1904 and 1913 as a result of which a number of educational conferences were planned to control the educational policy of the country for the first time. A National Council of Education was established in Bengal to reform the educational system of the country. Simultaneously, efforts were made by G.K. Gokhale and other Indian reformers to introduce compulsory education in India but Central Legislation rejected the proposals outright.

All India Conference

The first All India Conference on Education was convened by Lord Curzon in 1901 and an Educational Policy was published in 1904 in the form of a government resolution. It made valuable suggestions and accepted in principle that the government should not enter into competition. The government should exercise general control over all public institutions through Inspectors appointed by it so that the system could function efficiently.

Membership in Viceroy's Council

Between 1906 and 1920, a number of circulars on the improvement of primary education, abolition of fee in primary schools, training of teachers, textbooks preparation and the education of girls, etc. were issued to State governments. In 1910, it was decided to add a Member for Education in the Viceroy's Executive Council. The Bureau of Education was established in 1915 which was given the responsibility of keeping the records of the proceedings of meetings and to compile educational information besides other executive duties.

Other Reforms

The National Council of Education was set up by people like Rashbehari Ghosh and R.N. Tagore which sought to spread education amongst the masses. In 1912, the Central Government provided funds to institutions for the construction of buildings and setting up of libraries, laboratories and purchase of equipment, etc. to encourage efficiency and to provide education to the masses.

Gokhale's Scheme

The Education Policy of 1904 stated that the "rapid spread of primary education is one of the foremost duties of the State". As a result of Gokhale's attempts to introduce free and compulsory primary education in India, the Indian National Congress and the Muslim League passed resolutions in 1910 to this effect.

On 16 March 1911, G.K. Gokhale introduced a bill in the Imperial Legislative Council, stressing the role of local bodies in the areas under their respective jurisdiction to apply their discretion after seeking government consent for the enforcement of the Act. The opinions of state governments, universities and some institutions were sought and in 1912, the bill was referred to a select Committee but the bill was rejected. Even then it had its impact and the government realized the need for extending elementary education in the country.

Resolution on Educational Policy

The Government of India passed a Resolution on Educational Policy in February 1913 in the nature of an interim report. Many shortcomings and defects prevalent in the Indian educational system were pointed out in the report. The resolution stressed the need of educating boys and girls equally. It was stressed that teachers be provided orientation from time to time and a proper curriculum each for boys and girls be designed separately. This reference about training of teachers had never been taken up so seriously earlier. Suitable provision of grants-in-aid was recommended for private schools.

World War I and After

World War I provided a setback to the development of education and expansion programmes of school education, as suggested in the resolution, due to lack of funds but the number of students and institutions grew significantly.

The Education Department at the Centre took effective steps and devised strategies for spreading women's education. Many schools, run by local bodies were transferred to the government. Adequate arrangements for conveyance were made for the girls and separate schools for boys and girls started functioning. In 1904, the Central Hindu Girls' School at Banaras was started by Annie Besant. Owing to the outbreak of World War I, the people took the initiative in sending their children to school but the Civil Disobedience Movement, the economic depression all over the world, and the spread of epidemics halted the initiative. As a consequence of the Montform Reforms of 1919, it became obligatory on the part of the government to frame policies for the entire country. The Central Advisory Board of Education was set up in 1921. The main function of the Board was to give expert advice on all important matters concerning education but the Board and the Bureau of Education were disbanded after two years i.e in 1923, due to financial constraints. The Hartog Committee suggested the revival of the Board which came into being in 1935 and the Bureau of Education was also revived in 1937.

Sapru Committee Report

The UP Government under P.N. Sapru appointed a committee to enquire into the causes of unemployment. The committee concluded that the aim of the system of education imparted to the pupils was to pass examinations and not for a vocation. Its main recommendations were as follows:

- Introduction of diversification of courses at the secondary stage of education.
- Abolition of the intermediate stage and extension of one year at the secondary stage and the secondary stage of six years'

duration-three years for the lower stage and three years for the upper secondary stage.

- Introduction of vocational training after the lower secondary stage.

CABE Resolutions

The Central Advisory Board of Education (CABE) passed the resolution in 1935 that the primary stage should provide a minimum of general education and training ensuring literacy while at the lower secondary stage, specialized practical courses should be organized. At the higher secondary stage, the students were to be mainly prepared for admission to universities for imparting training of teachers in rural areas and specialized training in technical subjects and agriculture.

Abbott and Wood Committee

The Government of India invited A. Abbott and S.H. Wood to seek their expert advice on the reorganization of education in India. They submitted their report in 1937. The important recommendations of the report were as follows:

- Infant classes should be taken by trained teachers only. There should be greater emphasis on women's education to achieve this objective.
- Education in the primary classes should be related to the natural interests and activities of the children rather than to textbooks.
- The education of rural middle schools should be related to the natural environment.
- Upto the high school stage, the medium of instruction should be preferably the mother tongue of the child but English should be compulsory.
- There should be a three-year course for the teachers of primary and middle schools.
- General and vocational education should be interlinked.

It is perhaps most significant to point out that in his noting (file available with National Archives), Lord Curzorn had remarked: "That so far as the National Policies of Education in India is concerned, we as Britishers have to see our interest of UK".

National Movement on Education

Gandhiji had published his article of educational ideals in the "Harijan" in which he advocated universal compulsory education for all children between six to 13 years of age. He was of the view that true education should be self-supporting and the medium of instruction should be the mother tongue with emphasis on craft. He preferred relevant reconstruction of education for the rural children.

Zakir Husain Committee

The Indian National Conference held in 1937 constituted a committee under the chairmanship of Dr Zakir Husain who submitted a scheme in February 1938, known as the Wardha Scheme. The main recommendations of the Committee were:

- to impart education through some vocation;
- to be self-supporting which could cover teachers' salaries and also make pupils self-supporting;
- every person must learn to earn his living through education and dignity of labour to be maintained;
- instruction was to be related to the child's immediate environment. Instead of English, Hindustani was to serve as the national language.

The Zakir Husain Committee Report provided a plan of 'Basic' Education incorporating the Gandhian philosophy of education. This plan is also known as Nai Talim or 'new education'. The Report was criticized by many as it laid too much emphasis on basic craft. The report, however, made a significant dent on the modern educational thought of India.

Sir John Sergeant Report

The Government of India appointed Sir John Sergeant to prepare a scheme on Post-War Educational Development in India. The scheme was published in the form of a report which provided a reasonable provision of pre-primary education for children between the ages of three and six; universal compulsory and free primary education for all children between the ages of six and 14: secondary education for six years for the selected children in the age group of 11 to 17. Adult education for the age group of 10 to 40 years of age for nine crore illiterates and provision for comprehensive training to all the teachers; special schools for children suffering from mental and physical handicaps. Setting up of a strong education department at the Centre, and creation of an employment bureau were the other recommendations of the Sergeant Report. In the meantime, all State Departments appointed their own reorganization Committees and published reports for implementation.

Education in Free India

In September 1945, the Government of India created a separate Department of Education at the Centre and strengthened the Bureau of Education. In 1947, when India attained freedom, it was felt that the right type of education to suit people's aspirations was required as the existing institutions were closely associated with the British. National schools were started with the difference that in place of English, Hindi was introduced as the mother tongue and medium of instruction.

The Government of India set up a separate Ministry of Education which was bifurcated after a decade and known as the Ministry of Education and the Ministry of Scientific Research and Cultural Affairs. After five years, it was again amalgamated and known as the Ministry of Education. After a gap of nearly 23 years, it has become a Department of Education in the Ministry of Human Resource Development at the Centre and a separate Ministry practically in all the states and union territories. In free India, education is the responsibility of the Central Government, State Governments and the local bodies. The Central Advisory Board of Education is the main body at the centre which is constituted by representatives from the State Governments/union territories with the Union Minister of Education or the Minister of Human Resource Development as its Chairperson.

Tarachand Committee

The Government of India in 1948-49 appointed a committee with Dr Tara Chand as its Chairman to examine the problems of secondary education. The following were the main recommendations of the Committee.

- Secondary schools should be of multi-lateral type.
- The teaching of federal language shall be a compulsory subject at the secondary stage.
- There shall be one examination at the end of the secondary stage.
- The pay and service conditions of teachers should be as recommended by the Central Advisory Board of Education.

The Mudaliar Committee

To bring about the improvements and reorganization in the prevailing system of secondary education in the country, the Government of India appointed the Secondary Education Commission with Dr. A. Lakshmanaswani Mudaliar as its Chairman in September 1952. The report was submitted in June 1963. The main recommendations of the Committee were:

- Secondary education should commence after four or five years period of primary education and duration of the higher secondary stage should be four years. The intermediate stage should be replaced by the higher secondary stage.
- The first degree course should be of three years' duration.
- Provision of more schools for the age group of 14-17, upgrading of high into higher secondary schools, conversion of high schools into multi-purpose schools and provision of adequate supply of teachers.

The Kothari Commission

In July 1964, the Government of India appointed a commission with Dr D.S. Kothari as its Chairman. The Commission was entrusted with the task of making a comprehensive review of the entire educational system with emphasis on the development of education at all steps and in all its aspects. The Commission submitted its report to the Government of India in 1966.

The report of the Kothari Commission mainly dealt with the internal transformation of the educational system so as to relate it to the life, needs and aspirations of the nation, bringing out qualitative improvements of education and expansion of educational facilities on the basis of manpower need and with an accent on equal educational opportunities.

The Commission suggested that education should be linked to productivity. To achieve this objective, it is essential that science education, work experience, vocationalization and environment, etc. become an integral part of education in schools. It laid emphasis on the provision of more budget on priority basis. Social and National Integration should become the major objective of the educational system for which it is necessary to introduce a Common School System, and Social and National Service. Mother tongue should be the medium of instruction and textbooks on scientific and technical subjects be in respective regional languages. The teaching of English may be continued in all Indian institutions but Hindi be considered in due course. The education system should lay emphasis on the development of social, moral and spiritual values and for this purpose it was necessary for the Central Government, the State Governments and privately managed institutes to adopt the required measures. The new educational structure should be:

- One to three years of pre-school education.
- A ten-year period of general education which may be seven to eight years into the primary stage (a lower primary stage of four or five years and higher primary stage of three or two years), lower secondary stage of three or two years of general education; one to three years of vocational education and higher secondary stage of two years of general education or one to three years of vocational education.
- The age of admission to Class I should not be less than six.
- The first public external examination should be at the end of the first ten years of school while secondary schools should be of two types, viz. high schools providing ten-year courses and higher secondary schools providing a course of 11 to 12 years.
- Intensive and continuous efforts were needed to raise the economic, social and professional status of teachers and to bring talented young persons into this profession by laying down the minimum pay scales for teachers. It recommended three main scales for teachers, i.e. (a) those who have completed the secondary school stage and are trained, (b) for trained graduates, and (c) for teachers with post-graduate qualifications with promotional prospects and other benefits. It suggested that early steps be taken for improving the training institutions for teachers by laying down standards, and for providing substantial funds.
- The National Enrolment Policy should provide effective general education of not less than seven years' duration to every child and strive to equalize educational opportunity. There should be good institutes for the education of handicapped children and efforts should be made to bring in as many children as possible. It is necessary to give adequate attention to the education of girls at all stages, and to other deprived sections, viz. backward classes, tribal people, etc.

- The commission recommended that the objective of primary education should be to prepare individuals to be responsible and useful citizens and the constitutional directive of providing free and compulsory education for every child upto 14 years is an educational objective. School curriculum should be revised periodically, based on research in curriculum development; teaching learning materials be developed to provide necessary support and the teachers be provided orientation through in-service education programmes. The commission laid more emphasis on teaching methods, guidance, physical facilities and evaluation procedures which need to be considered seriously and suggested improvements in examination and internal assessment methods. It also provided that 90 per cent of India's rural population have a school within a radius of one kilometre.

The other important development has been the acceptance and implementation of the 10+2+3 system of education. The Kothari Commission report made a significant dent in the history of education. There was an amendment in the Constitution in 1976 and education was included in the Concurrent list which implies sharing of financial and administrative responsibilities between the Centre and the States.

In order to attain for the people the benefits of new opportunities in the changing environment, the perceptions which contribute towards creativity, the scientific temper and independence of mind are to be developed in them. There has been considerable enrolment of students and many new educational institutions have come into being but the rapid increase has outnumbered the educational inputs provided since Independence. Also, the financial outlays for education have been considerably decreased and still going low.

In the first Five Year Plan, the total outlay for education was 8.7 per cent, for the second Plan it was 6.3 per cent, for the third Plan 6.7 per cent, the fourth Plan provided for 5.1 per cent whereas for the fifth Plan it was 4.6 per cent. In the ninth Plan, it aimed to attain the outlay for education at 6.7 per cent.

National Policy on Education-1986

The National Policy on Education-1986 strives to fulfill the following objectives.

It is realized that education is an investment in the development of human resources. The policy aims to design the curriculum at all stages to create a rich cultural heritage to formulate schemes for the Scheduled Castes, Scheduled Tribes and to provide incentives in keeping with their needs. Adequate measures are to be provided to give vocational training to the disabled and other handicapped people. Mass literacy programmes of gigantic nature, especially for the age group of 15-35 years, shall be carried out to eradicate illiteracy. There would be basic facilities in the primary schools under Operation Blackboard. For school drop-outs, a large number of programmes of non-formal education shall be implemented. A massive organization of training for five lakh school teachers each year was organized in 1986, 1987, 1988 and 1989. Vocational courses are to be run by the public sector and the private sector to meet the needs of rural and tribal people, women and other deprived sections of the society. There would be a technology mission launched for radio, ETV broadcasts and other communication channels through Insat for students, teachers and the community, especially for rural areas.

Science education which aims at defining values such as creativity, objectivity and curiosity shall be encouraged. With the introduction of computers in schools, children shall be able to understand the relationship between cause and effect and the role of other variables. The examination system shall be redesigned to bring about qualitative improvement in education and would eliminate the element of chance and discourage rote memory. The teachers' recruitment shall be reorganized and efforts would be made to motivate and inspire teachers on constructive lines so that they devise new and appropriate methods of communication, and materials for the learners.

District Boards of Education shall be created to manage the educational set-up at the district level with the community having a leading role.

In 1990, the Government of India appointed a committee, with Shri Ram Murti as its Chairman, to review the National Policy on Education-1986 and to make suitable recommendations on restructuring the present education system. Comments were invited from premier educational institutions like NCERT, NIEPA, and the SCERTs for the implementation of the National Policy on Education. The report of the task force on the preparation of a Programme of Action (POA) was submitted in 1992 which includes among other things the formation of a task force for the use of the media and educational technology related to the curriculum as well as enrichment-curriculum-based school education.

Policy statements in the National Policy on Education-l 986 provide for the employment of educational technology to reach out to the most distant areas and the most deprived sections of the beneficiaries, simultaneously with the areas of comparative affluence in order to improve the quality, create an awareness of art and culture, and inculcate abiding values both in the formal and non-formal sectors.

The National Policy on Education also provides for reviewing and updating of the curriculum. It is in this context that the National Curriculum Framework for School Education was developed by NCERT. The document was released in November 2000 and subsequently in 2005. The policy document touches the vital issues of secularism, national integration, value education and their relevance to the educational processes. The Curriculum Framework has also stressed the need to face the new emerging challenges of various influences of globalization in India in the National Curriculum Framework, 2005.

According to the reports (The Hindustan times dated 6 Sept., 2016), it is evident from the current trend that India will be half century late in achieving its global education commitment as per UNESCO Reporter the Global Education Monitoring (GEM) report states that based on current trends, India is expected to achieve universal primary education in 2050; universal lower secondary education in 2060, and universal upper secondary education in 2085. This inplies that it would be more that half a century from the 2030. Goals (SDG) Sustainable is the deadline. But all the efforts seem to offset by the higher population growth and all the matching infrastructure and materials are not able to cope with the rising trend of population. However, the use of latest technologies in education seem to be the positive feature to fulfil this task. The National Curriculam Framework, 2017 is being finalised for circulation among the teachers and educationists of India for their valuable comments.

□

9

AUDIO-RADIO PROGRAMS FOR EDUCATION

Audio-radio is the most important media of mass communication throughout the world. Educational broadcasts are generally part of the programs, produced in a radio station. In such types of programs, there is a direct and face-to-face communication. In ratio broadcasts, messages are coded by using sounds which are both verbal and non-verbals. These sounds are transmitted to the listeners who listen and then interact for effective communication. While designing the message for audio-radio programs, the profile of the listeners such as age, socio-economic factors and his/her environment is the main consideration.

Educational radio broadcasts started during the First World War and expanded very rapidly. Practically, all the states have been producing educational programs in their regional languages under the control of Prasar Bharti. The types of educational programs being produced and broadcast are school broadcasts, university broadcast. Broadcasts for correspondence and non-formal education through IGNOU known as Gyan Vani, besides the Community Radio Broadcasts covering upto 10-12 km area of operation.

Audio-Radio Programme Production The Process

Of all the mass media, radio is perhaps the most simple medium. It is highly flexible. It is instant and immediate. The most striking feature of the audio-radio medium is its simplicity. In fact, radio is the simplest medium in so far as its production, broadcast and reception systems are concerned.

The Radio Production System

In its simplest form, we know that even a one-man production team is often capable of producing a good number of audio-radio programmes provided one has handy access to well-prepared scripts on a regular basis. Such audio-radio programmes may be wanting in professional standards yet these can be gainfully utilised by students and teachers.

It must, however, be accepted that quality of media programmes depends largely on a well-organised production system supported by good quality technical equipment and well-trained technicians and producers. One may have a first rate programme script and fantastic professional voices to record it. But if the equipment is below professional standards and the operational techniques are poor, the end-product is likely to be a disaster.

In the audio-radio medium, the listeners are wholly dependent on sound. If the recorded sounds are distorted, jarring and confused, the listeners will find the programme boring and uninteresting. In any production system, small or big, therefore, the final programme quality must get the uppermost priority. This condition presupposes a well-organised audio-radio production system supported by high quality equipment, trained producers and technicians all operating in a professionally conducive, healthy and stimulating environment.

Among the notable efforts in ET has been the Radio Pilot Project of the CIET in which radio was systematically and successfully used in teaching Hindi as first language to the children of class I, II and III of 500 villages in Rajasthan, wider use of radio lessons for teachers produced by CIEF Hyderabad (Central Institute of English and Foreign Languages) and training of a large number of teachers of Kerala through radio. Also appropriate multimedia packages as enrichment material for use of elementary classes (both formal and non-formal education) were prepared and disseminated with lot of audio component. For effective impact, the use of educational audio media was integrated with the system. It also used educational broadcast to support non-formal system of education for out of school children and enriching the system by broadcasting programs to fill up instructional gaps by providing educational experience which the classrooms teacher may not be able to provide. Designing and preparing of quality audio software is a time consuming teamwork which needs immediate insight into the process of communication. Also audio software can promote learning and motivate the learners.

Developing Programme Briefs for Educational Scripts

Media programmes generally originate from an idea or a theme. Identification of ideas and themes is, therefore, the basic step in the scheme of media programme planning and production. Once accepted, programme ideas and themes are further analysed, researched and expanded into what may be called "a program brief" or a programme outline.

Often, this outline is sufficient for the scriptwriter and the producer to design a script around it. However, a more standardized procedure for developing detailed programme briefs on several scripts, is followed in organisatons engaged in large-scale-production and regular broadcast of programme.

A programme brief is a written, typed or printed statement of intent. It serves as a basic document for providing all related information, ideas, sources and suggestions arranged coherently at one place. Producers, researchers and scriptwriters can freely draw upon such prepared materials to design scripts and programmes.

There is no standard format for designing programme briefs. Usually, however, a programme brief for a radio or television programme should inciude the following information:-

- Series Title
- Programme Title (working title only)
- Target Audience
- Programme Length or Duration
- Programme Objectives (stated in behavioural terms)
- Brief Content Outline
- Suggested Treatment and Possible Production Resources.

Sometimes detailed programme briefs are designed jointly by a team consisting subject experts, curriculum planners, researchers, educators, communication specialists, scriptwriters and producers. Programme brief, serve as basic reference materials for scriptwriters, producers and researchers. In fact, programme briefs bind scriptwriters and producers to follow a given mandate and help them remain on track while designing as, script or producing the final programme.

Presentation Formats for Radio/Audio Programmes

Radio programme writers and producers use a variety of formats for presentation of their programmes. These formats are common to radio, television and film, but each medium adapts a particular format for better impact and communication. For educational radio progammes, we may choose to use a particular format or a combination of two or more formats which suit our requirements. The decision to select a particular format or a combination of formats, is generally guided by the following factors:

- Nature of the specific subject matter to be dealt with or presented in the programme.
- Objectives of the programme stated in behavioural terms.
- Characteristics and interests of the target audience.
- Time and production resources available to the script writer and the programme producer.

Some of the commonly used formats for presentation of educational radio and video programmes are described below:

(i) **Story/Straight Talk:** More suited to radio programmes, the straight talk or the story format generally uses one person as a narrator. Illustrated talks, specially recorded reports and newscasts are covered under this category. To add a little variety, sometimes two persons/voices are used for presentation of the desired materials. Fully scripted in advance, stories and talks are often used for presenting a variety of educational materials through radio and are generally liked by young children.

(ii) **Interview:** In this format, two people an interviewer and an interviewee are engaged in a face-to-face dialogue. The interviewer talks to the interviewee on behalf of the listeners and attempts to elicit from the interviewee interesting information relevant to the topic under discussion. Interview format is useful for presenting programmes on current affairs or such informational and educational programmes in which a living scholar, scientist or an expert talks to the audience, enhancing the interest and the credibility of the presentation. Interviews are generally not scripted. Room opening and concluding questions and remarks are written down sometimes. The rest of the programme is extempore and unscripted and much depends on the interviewer's confidence, skill and home work. Relevant questions framed with clarity, arranged logically and asked with confidence, tact and spontaneity, are the heart of a good radio interview.

(iii) Panel Discussion : This is an extension of the interview format. Here, a select panel consisting of three or more experts discusses some subject-matter of educational interest. A panel discussion brings people of different opinions and viewpoints on one platform. The panel chairman guides and moderates the discussion. It requires no script but the moderator or the host should do thorough homework. He should be very alert, well-informed and tactful and should remain in full command of the situation to ensure cordial, orderly and meaningful discussion.

(iv) Dialogue: The dialogue is similar to the discussion. Like the interview, it involves two people who are experts in the same field. There are no questions and answers, nor there is a chairman. The two people involved in the dialogue, present similar and complementary views on the subject under discussion, each supporting the other. The whole atmosphere is relaxed as opposed to a discussion or an interview where participants may have opposing views and atmosphere may get charged.

(v) Actuality: Actuality means the "live" recording of a real event taking place any where. An effective and credible format in itself, actuality can form part of any other format, specially newscasts.

(vi) Feature: In this format, a single topic or subject is chosen for presenting its various aspects facts, opinions, beliefs, arguments, can counter-arguments-all about the same topic.

(vii) Magazine: The term magazine comes from the print medium. Just as a weekly or fortnightly magazine section of a newspaper or publication contains articles on different topics; a radio magazine programme can also have different kinds of items, often unrelated. The difference between a 'magazine' and a 'feature' is that the former covers a variety of subject areas in the same programme; whereas the latter deals with various aspects of the same topic. A magazine programme is like a visit to a fair or a departmental store where we find a variety of materials for a host of visitors or audience groups. The magazine programme can hold the attention of viewers longer because of its variety.

(viii) Drama: Essentially, drama is a literary form of story-telling. Radio has borrowed this format directly from the theatre. Drama is a very interesting and entertaining format and is specially effective when it is intended to appeal to the emotions of the audience. Radio drama enables us to present and watch people's behaviour, temperament and characteristics in realistic or life-like situations. Writing and producing a good radio drama is a difficult task. Nevertheless, numerous educational topics in history, literature, social sciences and other areas, lend themselves to perfect dramatic adaptation and presentation. Radio drama is acted out by a cast of special drama voices and wholly depends on sounds, sound effects, dialouges and music to create the mood and situations.

(ix) Documentary: As opposed to drama, the documentary format takes a factual approach to a subject. Here, an issue is treated in depth investigating all its aspects factually. The main emphasis in a documentary is on documenting real life, real people, real events, real places, real sounds and real experiences of people. A documentary maker's main job is to research and investigate various aspects or the topic factually and in depth. He uses a variety of techniques for presenting his materials, e.g. narration, montage, interview, discussions, eye-witness accounts, even "man-in-the-street" comments and expert's opinions-all put together in a logical way. The documentary format is suitable for presentation of current events and past happenings social, political and historical.

(x) Quiz: It is a useful format for presenting educational and current affairs programmes on radio. Quiz format is highly stimulating and participatory. It holds the attention or the viewers, keeps them active and fully involved and engrossed in the prograrnmc. It may be mentioned that most of the above formats are used independently as well as in combination with one or more formats and techniques, depending on the choice or the programme writer and producer. The choice of the format or a combination of formats, however, again depends on the nature and objectives of the specific subject matter and availability of time, budget and resources.

Nature of Sound Its Component and Characteristics

It is very important for programme writers and producers to understand the nature of sound, its components and characteristics.

The non-visual nature of radio is its real strength. The radio writer and producer can create fantastic pictures in listeners' minds by using powerful words and commentary and by combining dialogue, sound effects, music, noises and even silences. What is shown on television or film through elaborate studio settings, tedious and time-consuming computer animations and complex visual actions, can be presented on radio with great care by making intelligent use of words, dialogues, music, sound effects, and noises. Such is the power and magic of sound which audio-radio medium is made of.

Broadly speaking, the sound has the following components:

1. **Voice:** Human voice is by far the most important element of sound. It can take several forms such as dialogues, monologues, straight talk or narration, commentary, recital or recitation. It may also include animal voices.

2. **Music:** It includes background music, theme music, other kinds of suggestive music-happy, hilarious or sinister.

3. **Sound Effects:** It includes all kinds of sound effects, both original as well as specially recorded, such as atmospheric sound effects, sounds of rain, footsteps, winds, fire, explosions, traffic sounds and all kinds of peculiar or sudden noises.

4. **Silence:** It includes sudden silences that create impressions of stillness, peace, death, doom, etc. A combination or blending of several sound elements music, effects etc. is sometimes used to enrieh and emphasise the desired meaning and impact.

Knowledge of the nature of sound, its various components and characteristics, is essential for the writers and producers of audio-radio programmes. In so far as the designing and production of educational programmes is concerned, the medium of sound does offer immensly rich and limitless possibilities with much less cost.

Script Writing Guidelines/Tips

TARGET AUDIENCE: knowing them, their previous knowledge

OBJECTIVES: What is the objective of the programme

CONTENT What and how much the message should go

- Get to know your subject thoroughly. Read and ask questions. Dig, probe and search.
- Write down all the things the programme must cover. Get
- feedback from others and revise it.
- Be concise, do not try to stretch it out; use short, simple words and sentences.
- Use non-technical words common words also wherever possible. Define any jargon that may be foreign/new to the audience.
- Do not jump from one idea concept to another without a transition.

Make processes steps clear-say

1. first. ....second .... third ....
2. to start with......................then .... finally ....

- Always think and visualize first. It will help you to cut down on audio.
- Repetition and review are good for educational programmes but over-doing can make it boring.

Be prepared to make changes in the script.

Elements of a Good Script

- An attractive start
- Clarity of concept
- Known to unknown approach
- Interactive in nature
- Simple language
- No tricks, easily understandable technique
- No ambiguity
- Smooth transition
- Component of humour/fun
- Re-inforcement
- Smooth close down

Gyan Vani

Prasar Bharti, All-India Radio have allotted 38 Stations of FM to IGNOU for broadcasting audio programmes. Three station in Southern Region for Gyan Vani are being created, especially in collaboration with the All-India Radio by IGNOU. However, NCERT's programmes are already being aired by 10 stations of the AIR once a week in the Hindi-speaking belt.

1. Allahabad
2. Bhopal
3. Delhi
4. Indore
5. Jaipur
6. Jodhpur
7. Lucknow
8. Patna
9. Rohtak
10. Shimla

To cope with FM mode of broadcast, the stereo-mode of recording is essential whereas, NCERT is now having the digital system in the CIET since the broadcast system in the country has been mono. To be abreast with the latest development and produce quality programme stereo-recording equipment is needed. The other quality measures, stated for television, in terms of quality control, research evaluation are applicable alike to audio/radio programmes also. This has now been accomplished by the NCERT.

□

10

(A) SATELLITE INSTRUCTIONAL TELEVISION

Experiment

Television service in India was inaugurated on 15 September 1959 on an experimental basis in the 30 schools of Delhi Education Department. A new era in the history of television in India started in 1975 when the satellite was used on an experimental basis for instructional purposes.

Research studies reveal that when combined with other learning experiences Television has proved to be an effective tool. In fact, it was the vision of Dr. Vikram A. Sarabhai, an eminent scientist of India that if the rural/backward areas are to be covered by television satellite is the only alternative as low power and high power transmitters have their limited reach.

The Satellite Instructional Television Experiment (SITE) was a unique experiment in the realm of education and communication, not only in India but perhaps throughout the world which contributed to our education in many ways and many educationalists and communication experts are well aware of this development. In the area of instructional. TV, the then Ministry of Education (Now MHRD) sponsored four studies of the programs transmitted to the selected primary schools in the states of Andhra Pradesh, Karnataka, Rajasthan and Orissa although the experiment was conducted in six states Andhra Pradesh, Bihar, Karnataka, Madhya Pradesh, Orissa and Rajasthan. Under this experiment instructional TV programs were transmitted via a satellite to nearly 2400 villages. This experiment commenced on 1 August 1975 and ended on 31 July 1976.

Through satellite, it became possible to take TV to the villages of India for the first time before it reached metropolitan cities covered under normal expansion of TV. programs. The areas selected for the programs were very remote and very poorly served by any media of communication. The most important objective of the experiment was to access the efficacy of T.V. as a medium of communication to supplement the educational content for national development. The programs were transmitted in the morning and in the evening as per the intergrated schedule. The morning transmissions were educational in character and intended for the school children while the aim of the evening transmissions was of general education and information nature for other sections of the audience. Expect on Sundays and school holidays the morning programs were transmitted daily for 22½ Minutes from 10-22 ½ AM to 10:45 AM.

The self-contained capsules ready for transmission were sent in advance to the Indian Space Research Organisation (ISRO), Ahmadabad for transmission through the satellite. The satellite beamed the programs to direct reception sets installed in the primary schools. In addition the Space Application Centre (SAC), ISRO produced 160 science programs which were broadcast to all the six states covered by the experiment. ISRO Science programs were telecast as SAC-SITE programs. Besides the programs produced by the Centre for Educational Technology (CET) - Dept of Teaching Aids (DTA) and the State Educational Technology Units and Doordarshan were also transmitted. ISRO programms were transmitted in all the states in dubbed language versions.

For the first time in the history of India new audience poorly served by the modern media and communication were brought face-to-face with T.V. medium under SITE. For one year instructional and educational programs on the theme of national development and education were .... continuously seen through the moving images and other multimedia-packages with the following objectives:

(i) To make the children sensitive to and learn education living skills.

(ii) To improve the basic concepts and skills in the areas of numeracy, literacy and technology.

(iii) To instill habits of hygiene and healthy living.

(iv) To promote aesthetic sensitivity.

(v) To make them aware of the process of modernization of life and the resultant changes in their attitudes.

Comprehensive list was provided to the production centres to serve as a pool for the selection of topics.

In the primary schools a mixed group of children between the ages 6 to 12 years, and their teachers watched instructional TV for the first time in their life. The teachers had been asked to prepare, receive and use this medium by a three-day orientation course. The course concerned itself with the logistics of seating children, the handling of the TV set and with the conducting of pre- and post-TV discussions. Teachers were also provided daily schedules of TV and teaching notes to assist them in better use of the telecasts. The ET. Cells of the State Govt. concerned arranged the training of teachers by C.E.T.N Delhi. The programs included the topics finalized in consultation with the State Education Departments of six satellite states. The programs produced and the formats adopted were on chorus songs, teaching of national anthem "features quiz, group dance, rural sports, documentary film etc. The science programs produced by ISRO were telecast on Mondays and Thursdays.

Training of script writing for the production of TV programs was taken up by the CET of NCERT in collaboration with the Upgraha DD Kendra through a series of workshops. However it was evident that there was a dire need to study the interaction between electronic medium, viz. TV and the rural audience who had never been exposed to this medium earlier especially seeing, listening and reacting to the combination of all these methods which are used by educational TV.

Although SITE was a time bound experience, TV was supposed to be a powerful medium for national development. This being the major concern, feasibility of mass communication programe for instructional purposes and then use to improve educational processes was explored at the highest levels.

TV viewing a new medium of mid-seventies with a certain amount of novelty was attached to this medium. It was hoped that TV being a new mode of education and entertainment for the rural children would be an innovative device as it has the potentials of holding the attention and sustaining the interest of the rural children. There are other qualities and techniques in the use of TV programs which gives TV tremendous superiority and advantage TV in the reality of rural schools became the means of enhancing the process of teaching-learning. Quality programs with better utilization can provide a breakthrough in solving many of the problems of rural schools.

Acceptance of TV is a big benefit which is significant. If the early childhood students can begin to understand the meaning and potential of TV, the concept of isolation of rural school would disappear.

There is a need of caution. It is necessary to gauge as to how the new approach has been accepted by the new audience, i.e. among the children who were exposed to these programs. It appears easy to assess the impact of TV in many ways but it is equally important to see the view-points of the target audience. It was of interest to find that the acceptance by the children was much greater than the teachers. The responses of the teachers reveal the hold of traditional teaching methods and values and inability to think beyond the traditions.

There was, however, another set of teachers, dedicated and devoted ones who strongly felt that TV made better understanding of content and adds certain qualities which would not have been possible through normal educational methods.

The "INSAT FOR EDUCATION" Project in 1982 has been another land-mark in the wide use of educational technology especially the TV in India. It emphasized that the responsibility of planning and production of educational software should be the responsibility of educationalists themselves which was assigned a new role to the education sector. After the setting up of the CIET in 1984, State Institutes of Educational Technology (SIETs) were set in the six INSAT states with the production centers in Andhra Pradesh, Bihar, Gujarat, Maharashtra, Odisha and U.P. Similarly, State Educational Technology (ET) cells, were merged with State Audio-Visual Departments to boost the application of educational technology and to create a climate and infrastructure for the purpose. Seventh SIET was set up in Kerala in 1999 for the production and transmission of TV programs to supplement the learning content.

However, the functioning of SIETs as a consequent of the non-acceptance of Doordarshan to transmit ETV programs in the Hindi and in regional languages due to various factors gave a big jolt to the project of production and transmission of programs and largely due to the mushroom growth of TV channels competition, nature and quality of productions and lack of sensibility of the content of educational programs. It is a pity that TV came to India with educational programs which have gone in the background and their place is being taken by advertisements, feature films and entertainment. Education programs tend to be boring by nature. It is suggested that we may always add wit and humour animation and produce programs which are edutainment so that the children and teachers may weave them with the educational content.

Gyan Darshan And Gyan Vani

A new era was heralded on 26 January 2000 in the realm of Educational Television with a dedicated Educational Channel titled, "GYAN DARSHAN" offered to the country. For one month the test transmission was tried out and thereafter, initially 12 hours of telecast each day commenced, followed by 18 hours and from January 2000, this has become the dedicated 24 hours uninterrupted Educational Channel of the country.

The Central Institute of Educational Technology, a Constituent of the NCERT has been declared the nodal centre for feeding this dedicated National Educational Channel in the area of School Education. Thus, NCERT is an active partner in GYAN DARSHAN programmes and its is sharing a major transmission responsibilityes. The entire responsibility of Educational Programmes in the school sector is being channelized through NCERT, which is providing programmes everyday for more than six hours approximately. For this purpose, it is receiving programmes for half an hour for Tuesday, Thursday, Friday, Saturday and Sunday from National Institute of Open Schooling. Similarly, half an hour programme on Tuesday and Thrusday is being received from SIET, Lucknow and only once a week, for half an hour on Saturdays SIET, Patna is sending the programme. This process from SIETs UP and Bihar has stopped.

Quality of the programme demands technical excellence, accurate, correct and balanced facts and authentic contents, interesting presentation techniques and programme formats with a suitable pacing. The continuous research and evaluation helps in developing quality programmes and incorporating the latest development both technical and pedagogical engaging the creative production techniques. This also demands skilled, professionally trained manpower and a continuous in-service orientation of the staff.

(B) EDUCATIONAL TELEVISION

Educational TV came to India in October 1961 on a regular basis. Being a powerful medium of communication, it was basically introduced into the education system of India to inform, instruct, entertain, motivate and to make the teaching-learning effective as it has the capacity to transmit many kinds of orientating and guiding the subject content. TV could demonstrate the live experiments and moving objects and also reproduce the accurate record from the video tape/CD/DVDs. Subject matter taught by TV is usually retained as long or longer than the taught conventionally in classrooms and also in non-formal education.

INSAT for Education Project in 1982 is a great landmark in the wider use of education Technology in India and a new role was given to the educational sector. State Institutes of Educational Technology (SIET), were set up in seven states to produce their own educational TV programs in regional languages for transmission in their states by Doordarshan Kendras. Central Institutes of Educational Technology (CIET) was set up in 1984 to boost the application of ET. This was amply stressed in the "Report of Task Force on NCERT". Challenge of Education: A policy perspective and National Curriculum Framework, 2005 and also in documents of NCERT.

Availability of appropriate Transmission time and also the television sets, their maintenance and management has always been a great problem. Doordarshan has now practically stopped all the Edl. TV transmission due to the paucity of funds. Also there are problems of quality productions in the CIET and SIETs/ EMRC/AVRC:-There is a cut throat competition of programs being transmitted by a number of channels and education is getting a very low priority. The setting up of SIETs was a Centrally sponsored scheme for a fixed of time and the MHRD is with-drawing support of funds and infrastructure in the SIETs and other production centers. Two SIETs have been closed down while the remaining ones are struggling for finances to produce programmes. Doordarshan has completely withdrawn and the programs produced by the state/cultural funding production agencies of the school and higher education level are being transmitted by Gyan Darshan, IGNOU which have been provided uplinking facilities by ISRO. Also the programs produced by these agencies are openly available through Internet without any cost as these are the outcome from public funding but only for non-commercial use.

MHRD has stressed the need for the integrated plan for conceptualisation production, distribution, retrieval, utilization and feedback which is being conceived in higher circles. The idea of producing E-books has also been mooted. but it seems to be ill advised as the production of books through electronic media is a virtual misuse of media. What is required, a comprehensive plan to identify the difficult concepts from the conceptual materials and to produce animation based, through various formats, those programs which the target audience feel interested to see otherwise the average programs produced as proto-types are confined to the almirahs and hardly used in the institutions. Use of quality TV programs requiring teamwork, spirit of irrovation and vital linkages with the academic content are extremely important to accomplish this objective. It may also require new organizational structures and management strategies to be developed in the education system to promote the use of ETV.

Similarly, teacher training both pre-service and in service is a high priority area. ETV, being an integral part of teaching-learning material should be exposed to the teacher in their various teacher training programs so that they can use them effectively as part of pre- and post-telecast activities.

Production of quality programme would be futile exercise if the TV sets are not provided/made available in schools or there is no maintenance mechanism. An Impact Evaluation Study of the Centrally Sponsored Scheme of Education Technology under which nearly 60,000 TV sets supplied by the Govt. of India in 1987-88 confirm the fact that the TV sets and radio-cum cassette players supplied to the schools were not utilized effectively. The main reasons for non-utilisation were that the sets were not in working condition and there was no mechanism for repairs. Many sets were safely locked in the almirahs with the latent fear that the set might be stolen after use and the headmaster/headmistress is held responsible. There were schools where the sets were supplied but no electricity in the school. For increasing the TV programme there was no space in the school where screening could be arranged for 40-50 students. And above all this, there is no period earmarked for TV viewing in the school.

We may sum up saying that teleconferencing and interactivity are the two strong elements which can make a visible impact in our teaching-learning process.

TIPS FOR T.V. SCRIPT-WRITING

- Get to know your subject thoroughly. Read and ask questions. Dig, probe and search.
- Write down all the things the video programme must cover. Get feedback from others and revise it.
- Be concise, do not try to stretch it out; use short, simple words and sentences.

- Use non-technical words/common words also wherever possible. Define any jargon that may be foreign/new to the audience.
- Do not jump from one idea/concept to another without a transition.
- Make processes/steps clear by say

  i. First...........................second.............................third.

  ii. to start with ....then.........................finally.
- Always think visuals first It will help you to cut down on audio.
- Repetition and review is good for educational programmes but over doing can make it boring.
- Be prepared to make changes in the script.

SCRIPT FOR T.V./VIDEO PROGRAMME

No.	Visual	Spoken Word/Commentary	Remarks

The Language of Shots

The five basic shots most commonl y used in television are:

1. Close-up (CU)	This includes the top of the shoulder. Eyes come at top one third of the screen. Good for showing details of a character's face or object.
2. Medium Close-up (MCU)	Mid Close or Medium Close-up cuts chest at a man's coat pocket top edge. Shows more of a person. Used commonly for newsreader or presenter shots.
3. Mid Shot (MS)	MS or Medium Shot is cutting at waist showing half of the subject, whether standing or sitting. Used for establishing presenter or interviewee.
4. Medium Long Shot (MLS)	Cutting at knees-showing more than half the subject. Sometimes called a three-quarter shot.
5. Long Shot (LS)	Full figure this includes the background also. There is twice as much headroom as foot room. Used for artist, entrance and dancers. As shot of this size begins to show a scene in relation to the setting.

There are many more shots also:

1. Big Close-up (BCU)	Cut off the top of the head, not mouth or chin. Used when the director wants the expression on features of the subject to be highlighted to the exclusion of everything else.
2. Very Long shot/wide angle (VLS)/(WA)	Usually refers to an estabishing shot of the whole set. Position of the artiste depends on other elements in the set.

3. Two shot (TS)	Indicates to two people in the shot, similarly 3S, three people
4. Mid Two Shot (MID 2S)	Two people in the shot, framing till the waist.
5. Low Angle shot (L/A)	Looking up at the subject. Verticals are emphasised and the foreground dominates. Used for making the object appear bigger as the background.
6. High Angle Shot (H/A)	The Horizontal planes become more obvious, the verticals are shortened and the foreground becomes less significant.
7. Point of View Shot (POV)	A shot in which the camera takes the point of view of a character or subject in the scene.
8 . Over the Shoulder Shot (OSS)	A shot in which the main subject is soon with the back of another persons and shoulders in the foreground. Also called CROSS SHOT.

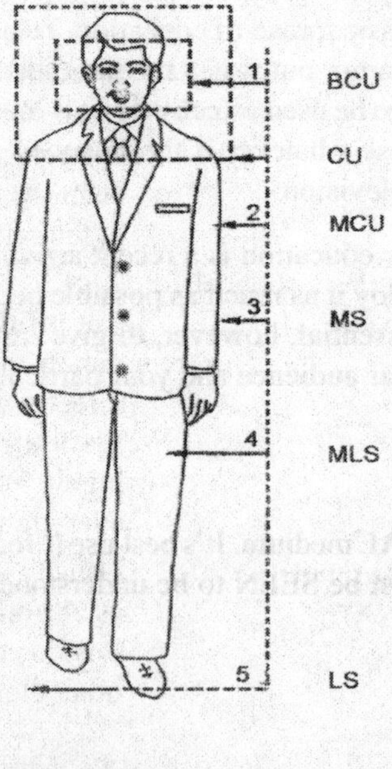

Time Line

Introduction Concept Concept 2, Revision and Sum up

....

Structure of a Video Programme

minutes Time Line ....

HOOK AND LINK	
Chain of Shots	Introduction transition Sequence I Advanced organisers Bridge Sequence-2 Transition Sequence -3 Bridge Summary

PRE-PRODUCTION-PLANNING -IDEA TO SCRIPT

Television is a medium that is becoming increasingly available in developing countries and is being explored as a possibility for the delivery of development messages or spread of education. Television has obvious visual advantages over radio, but it is a medium that requires a greater range of expertise if it is to be used effectively; it is much more expensive than radio and it is no use whatever if the intended audience does not have ready access to a television.

Where television for education is a recent arrival in a country, it is tempting to want to employ it as much as possible because it is a new or exciting medium. It is essential, however, to give careful consideration to its value for a particular audience and your particular message before you proceed with it.

Cautions

1. Television is a VISUAL medium. It's best use is for the dissemination of a message that must be SEEN to be understood and implemented effectively.

2. Using television requires completely different techniques from using radio. Too often where a radio writer/producer is expected to be able to transfer to television, there is tendency to write a script that is really "radio with pictures". The secret of television is to allow the picture to carry most of the message.

3. If you choose a visual medium, you must be sure you have something to SHOW throughout the full length of the program time.

4. You need a wide range of talanted people for production; writers; producers; cameramen; sound engineers; on air talent; lighting engineers; possibly make-up artists; graphics designer; editors; etc.

5. Television is a much more time-consuming production process than radio. Be sure that you have the necessary time available before you decide to use television.

(C) PRODUCTION OF E.T.V. PROGRAMES

In a television program for a development project three things must be matched up-the audio, the video and the message objectives. Objectives must come through clearly but must not misuse the medium. In other words, you should not be concerned with "getting the message across" that simply sit people in front of the camera and have them lecture on the message.

On the other hand, you must avoid letting the medium over-ride the message. Don't become so carried away with creating an interesting film that you allow the message to be swamped.

The creation of a good television program for a development is a delicately balanced affair, particularly when you remember that finished message also must be sufficiently culturally sensitive to your target audience, and that almost inevitably it will be made within a limited time frame and budget.

Components of a Good Television Program

A good television program must attract the audience's attention.

It will do this by being;

relevant to the audience

understandable

believable

technically well made

Attracting the Attention of an Audience

It is a good idea to give some thought as to what it is that attracts an audience to a subject particularly a subject with which they are not already familiar. Here are some suggestions you might consider.

Generally, people are attracted to something for one or more of the following reasons:

It affects their lives
It affects their health
It affects the welfare of their families
It offers an immediate (or near immediate) chance of increasing income,
It offers an immediate (or near immediate) chance of improving lifestyle
It allows them to make use of natural talent
It provides them with a feeling of self-worth
It gives pleasure
It is funny, odd or bizarre
They are introduced to it by a person they respect or like

On the other hand, people are generally not interested in or attracted to a subject that:

affects only other people
Is beyond their personal control
Will bring results only at some unidentifiable time in the future
Is difficult, confusing or expensive to carry out
Is offensive to their personal beliefs
Is too abstract in nature
- Is dull and boring and repetitive
- They are introduced to it by someone for whom they have neither respect nor liking.

With these considerations in mind, you can begin to prepare for using television as part of your project. Start by asking yourself these questions.

1. What are the special characteristics of television that make it worth considering as a major medium for your project?

2. What are the disadvantages of using television as a major medium for this project?

Main Television Program Types

1. Entertainment
2. News and documentary
3. Instructional/Informational
4. Edutainment

Characteristics of Effective Instructional/Informational Television Programs

1. Good Design: Purpose, objectives and message will be strong and clear throughout, and will be based on planning. There will be an effective balance of visual and aural presentation of the message, so that the visuals are not used as "decorative additions" to the spoken message.
2. Good Script: The message will be presented in a format suited to the medium and attractive to the chosen audience. At all times the script will acknowledge the importance of finding and maintaining the balance between message and medium.
3. Good Production: The finished program will be good, cleanly produced television, adhering to all the rules of good presentation both technically and artistically. The "instructional" nature of the program will not detract from the importance of first class production.

Classification of TV

TV is in terms of visuals spoken Programmes. It is viewed distinguishing between written and spoken words with supporting visuals in many forms such as dialogue, play, drama, story, poem, etc.

So TV programmes are mainly the visuals with spoken word programmes and or prose and music programmes. The programmes could be scripted or unscripted.

The selection of format depends not on novelty but on its suitability to express an idea to the audience.

FORMATS

Formats are audio visual cues with a special purpose in mind.

Writers write them into scripts,

Producers use them in direction/production

TV is distinguished from other media by its unique qualities and not by its content. These are:

Presentation techniques/communication skills

Comprehension of visuals

Sets and lighting

Strncture of the programme

Auditory features like sound effects

Laugh Tracks

Specialised dialogues

Musical Effects etc.

TIPS FOR WRITING T.V. SCRIPTS

1. Always ensure that characters are multi-dimensional. Not perfect human beings but models for our audience.
2. Make use of wit and humour, which allows us laugh together in a healthy way not at each other.
3. Conventional, informal language visuals are easy to relate than to preachy, perfectly structured sentences.
4. Include questions those asked aloud and those that children might think to themselves.
5. We should address our audience directly, involve them actively.
6. Encourage familiar story book 'coming alive through t.v., integrate message into folktale, songs, music, etc.
7. Use magazine format including story, narration, music, song, drama and explore how best use these formats so that children respond best and most effectively.

The message should get acrossed to children and to teacher.

GOOD CHILDREN T.V. PROGRAMMES SHOULD:

- Attract children's attention
- Present easily understood information

- With animation, puppets and story formats with wit and humour, children are generally fascinated
- Men's voice, long dialogues and content which goes above children's heads, discourages them to view programmes

BASIC AND PRIMARY CONSIDERATIONS

Target Audience : knowing them, their previous knowledge

Objectives : What is the objective of the programme

Content : What and how much the message should go

Critical stage of script development

* Interaction with script writer and the producer continues.

* Then technical script with story board visuals, locale and dialogues into logical sequences

This includes inter-relationship of all programme elements and resources

Feedback

Some Important points:

1. Observe uniform rules for script layout

(a) Always write speeches/dialogues on the right hand side of the page.

(b) Everything that is NOT to be spoken SHOULD BE WRITTEN IN CAPITAL LETTERS. (If you write in a language other than English, either use different inks, or underline the text which is not to be spoken.)

2. Television is a visual medium

In TV, the vision must come first, you must always remember and think of what the viewers will be looking at. So, make sure you exploit the visual potential of television drama, and describe visual sequence clearly in the script.

3. Don't use too many scene

Make use of several settings, but not too many. Always think of what is possible in your situation and write for scenes that are practical to construct in a studio or reach on a location.

4. Easiest drama is 'here and now'

TV deals with the 'here and now'. Any drama involving historical or super-natural scenes will be complicated and expensive to produce. Fantasy, for one thing, is out. (Cartoons and puppets are the only exception.) So, while writing for television drama, be realistic and stick to ordinary people in ordinary places.

5. ETV to restrict the number of speakers

TV is an intimate medium. Since the screen is so small, TV works mainly in close ups. So, never have more than for people in any scene and two or three is best of all.

The inherent power of the computers combined with the national reality reflected through television can improve the educational process. We can say that the marriage of computer with the television is the ideal solution to the problems of education today.

Focus group on Educational Technology in the NCERT gave a number of suggestions aimed at qualitative improvement of the school curriculum and evolved a large range of solutions. This includes the development of flexible systems, alternative subject contents, preparation and use of low cost expensive technological aids and continuous support system for teacher training with innovation resources to which the school could easily access to so that ET may be more relevant to enhance the process of learning as ET has the potentials to affect immediate reforms in the methods of teaching-learning accompanied through reformative and summulative methods of research.

We have a rich resource of trained manpower which could be reoriented and revitalized. There is a consciousness on the part of State Education Departments to research in the newer areas such as multi-media and interactive technology for which the rural/backward areas may be given top priority and involve the local education workers because the talent does not lie with the urban-based people only. There may be flexible approach in which various skills may be introduced such as reasoning and other skills of teaching learning. There has been strong feeling even among the teachers that media does not contribute to learning since they have never prepared any teaching-learning material and they are always scared of using the ready-made aids, brought from the market as they are not confident of using such aids. This outlook has to change. It is always challenging to encourage the use of flexible content and try out through the process of evaluation. To meet learner's needs is the first priority of teachers taking into account the availability of options with the teachers to solve their needs. This requires working out the new strategies/techniques and modern technologies which could be employed judiciously and appropriately to solve the various problems with which they are confronting.

(D) T.V. INTERVIEWING

TV interview is distinct from the word interviewing for the jobs appointment as both the interviewer and the interviewee are on equal footing.

The Interview – Sample Guidelines on the Program

1. An interviewer must be at ease, knowledgeable, vitally interested in the work of the person being interviewed, and professional in the conduct of the interview. Basically, an interview follows a question answer format with an introduction, main segment or body of information, and a conclusion. In style of performance it must be natural, straightforward and conversational.

2. The interview brings people from outside the radio station into programmes and it gives added human interest. The interview allows the broadcaster to ask questions for the audience. The interviewer represents the listener who, of course, can't ask questions themselves. The interview brings the experts, the well-known person and ordinary people into contact with the radio audience.

3. Of course, the interview is not the only way to bring outside people into a television programme. Other programme methods which do this are the talk, the discussion and the documentary.

Approach

4. Remember that a person does not have to give an interview. The station must obtain the co-operation of people. Wherever the interview takes place (whether in the studio or elsewhere), the interviewer is "not at home". When you are seeking knowledge , or information, or opinion, you are not on home ground. You should always be cautious when an another person's a territory.

5. Set a time for the interview — and be on time. If you're delayed, try to tell the person to be interviewed (telephone or send a

message).When asking a person for an interview, tell the person of the benefits of the interview being broadcast. The person should want to give the interview. You might have to persuade someone to be interviewed. If a person is worried about something, it's easy to say no.

6. If the interview is being recorded in someone's house or office, it may be necessary to re-arrange furniture (the ideal interviewing position varies according to the kind of micro-phone you use. Explain why you need to move furniture. Be polite. Every interview is important. Your actions should reflect this.

7. Be encouraging, particularly if you have to improve the performance of interviewee. You might have to ask the person to speak more loudly, to speak more slowly, or to say something in a different way. After the interview, some people like to hear the tape played back. If you can spare the time, it's friendly to agree to such a request. Thank the person generously but, at this stage, do not praise too highly. (You may find you need to heavily edit the interview or not even use it at all). If you are planning to edit, tell the interviewee what you're thinking of doing.

8. Be careful of saying definitely the time the interview will be telecast unless you're sure the recording is good, the interview is worth using and you have the authority to decide if it will be used.

9. After the telecast, tell the interviewee what you thought and what other people thought of the interview. It can be disappointing to do one's best and then have nobody notice.

What Makes a Good Interview?

10. A good interview is one that

    (a) Has a clear objective,
    (b) Is well researched and prepared,
    (c) Develops logically,
    (d) Keeps the audience involved,
    (e) Is impartial,
    (f) Is controlled by the interviewer,
    (g) Sounds conversational,
    (h) Is interesting.

11. You must know what you want to get from the person being interviewd,
    (a) information,
    (b) comment and opinion,
    (c) personal experience.
12. Limit your interview to one subject. Keep the reason for the interview clear in your mind. During the interview, if a second subject comes up, do another interview.

Research and Preparation

13. The best interviews are well researched and well prepared. Some necessary things to do:
    (a) Research the subject,
    (b) Research the interviewee
    (c) Prepare the questions.
14. **Research the subject.** Read papers, go to the library, look at an atlas, check with someone who knows, gather as much background information as you can. This will help you to ask intelligent and interesting questions. Before you start an interview you should already know quite a lot about the subject.
15. **Research the interviewee.** What do you know about the person you're going to interview? Consult written sources and people who know the person. Find out the person's age, interests, area of expertise, temperament. Check the person's voice. An interviewee may not be understood, if there is a heavy foreign accent or a speech defect. What do you call the person Sir, Doctor, Mister…..?
16. **Prepare the questions.** You must have a good idea of what you are going to ask. If your mind is blank, you can rely on who? What? When? Where? How? Followed by how much? How often? What effect?, etc. Prepare the questions so they are:
    (a) brief and to the point,
    (b) simple enough to be understood when first heard,
    (c) interesting,
    (d) single Questions (not two questions, otherwise it is unlikely that both will be answered).

(e) questions (not statements, although a statement followed by a question is a useful variation).

(f) not too informative (otherwise the interviewee will answer with a simple yes or no).

17. **Prepare possible answers.** The interviewer should never be caught off balance. Think of the kind of answer you will get. An interviewee's "line" is usually predicatable and plan the next question.

18. **Logical Development.** Ask questions in a logical order so the interview develops step by step. Plan a strong opening question (or, something, an easy opener and a strong follow-up). Plan a good last question so the interview ends on a high note. Logical does not mean inflexible. Be ready to change you questions or their order as the interview progresses. The end should be smooth.

19. **The Audience.** You interview on behalf of the listeners, so keep them in mind. Your audience may include many different kinds of people, or it may be a small and specialized group. You must know who your audience is. Keep the language clear and simple. Think of the "average" listener to the programme and ask questions for this person. Explain difficult or technical terms which the interviewee uses or ask the interviewee to explain them. Questions are based on what you think the audience wants to know.

20. The interview is a person to person situation but with both persons knowing there is an audience. If the audience does not understand or loses interest, the interview has failed.

21. **Impartiality.** The interviewer should not express a personal opinion in an interview. The interviewer represents the audience and the audience, taken together, has a wide opinion. Avoid making judgements. Your task is to get information or comment from other people so the listeners can make up their own minds.

22. **Keeping Control Pace.** Try to establish an even pace for the interview, not too fast, not too slow. Change the length of questions, some short, some long. Two or three short questions in a row will speed up an interview. Every good interview will have variety and contrast.

23. **Approach.** Try not to be frightened of the person you're interviewing. You can't control the interview if you're frightened. The opposite

approach, where the interviewer acts in a superior way, is bad mannered. The interview should be conversation between equals. Appear confident. If you feel nervous, try to hide it.

24. **Answer.** If you ask an important question and if the interviewee does not answer it properly, return to it.

25. **Interruptions.** You may need to interrupt an interviewee:
    (a) Who is talking too much,
    (b) Who is not very interesting,
    (c) Who is not talking about the subject,
    (d) When you feel more explanation is required.

26. It's hard to interrupt and be polite. But you can:
    (a) wait for a pause, then interrupt,
    (b) give some signal that you want to interrupt,
    (c) if all else fails, politely talk over the interviewee

("may I just interrupt and return to your comments on…?)

27. **Attentiveness.** In an interview you must listen twice as hard. That advice is for the interviewer, not the listener. You must listen to the interviewee and you must appear to be listening. Look the interviewee in the eyes. Be ready with the next question. Know when to stop the interview: when you've covered the subject when the interview has become uninteresting.

28. You must listen to the answers to your questions. If you don't you may well later ask a question which the interviewee has already answered. You may also miss out on a point which you should follow up.

29. **Ending.** When you end the interview, don't make an excuse. Leave thanks until after the recording is over.

30. **Losing control.** There are a number of ways in which an interviewee can cause you to lose control of an interview:
    (a) he can keep on talking (stop him politely and firmly),
    (b) he can stop talking (be ready with another question),
    (c) he can give you an uncomfortably short answer— "no" (be ready with a supplementary question—"and why not?"),

(d) he can ask you a question, unually seeking agreement with his point of view (side step and move on or ignore),

(e) he can get his facts wrong (edit later; if live interview, move on quickly),

(f) he can mispronounce a word that you must use again (when you have to use it, pronounce it correctly),

(g) he can pause as if finished and then start again just as you start the next question (give way),

(h) he can ask you to explain what you mean by a question (explain),

(i) he can object to your question (rephrase or move on, don't argue),

(j) he can become aggressive (never get involved in an argument).

31. **Conversational.** An interview is not conversation, but it sould look coversational, relaxed and friendly. For this reason, try to avoid:

(a) asking prepared questions one by one without any reference to what the interviewee is saying,

(b) written answers to prepare questions (this nearly always sounds "false"),

(c) rehearsing the interview in full (although it is useful to discuss the "line" of your questions with the interviewee),

(d) too much informality (this can make the audience feel left out—remember, the audience is always present).

32. **Interest.** Some interviewed sound uninteresting because:

(a) the speaker's voice is dull,

(b) the interviewer is not bright and lively,

(c) questions do not stipulate interesting answers,

(d) the interview is too long (a common fault).

33. The good interviewer encourages the person he is talking to by sounding and looking interested. This does not mean that the interviewer should interrupt with such expression as I see…… Ah……Mmmm………Is that so……… Yes…….. and so on. In fact, this is generally not desirable. A nod, a smile or an intelligent follow up question are better.

34. The interviewer can improve the interview by editing out the dull patches. But to have the feeling "I can always edit" shows bad planning. It also takes time to edit properly. After you have recorded the interview, sit alone and listen to it carefully. Ask yourself, how could I have improved it?

35. As a general rule, most interviews should not be longer than about five minutes. If the interview is very interesting, of course there is no reason why it should not go longer. Ask yourself the question, will the listeners be interested in hearing all of this? Better a five minute interview that everyone listen to than a 15 minutes interview that has few listeners after the first five minutes.

36. Interviewing outside the studio

Tape records. Before leaving the studio, check that:

(a) you have the microphone (and a wind guard if this might be necessary),

(b) the tape recorder does not have flat or near-flat batteries (take spares if you're not sure),

(c) microphone leads are not faulty (do a test recording and play back.

(d) recording performance is normal (no distortion, recorder at correct speed),

(e) you have enough erased tapes and tape lables,

(f) you have followed the recording stations rules for borrowing equipment.

37. Recording Place. Choose this carefully (if you have any choice). Try to find a quiet place where the sound quality (acoustic) not too bad.

38. Indoors. The interviewee will perform better in familiar surroundings, such as his office or home. Background noise can be controlled better indoors (you may need to take the telephone off the hook and stop the typewriters). In certain rooms you may get a lot of echo which spoils your recording.

This can be improved by:

(a) speaking in softer voices closer to the microphone,

(b) interviewing across the diagonal of the room (this reduces the direct reflection of sound).

39. **Outdoors.** You can get a more natural sound outside because there are no reflecting surfaces. However, there may be other problems. Wind can cause distortion (use a wind guard or, if you don't have one, a handkerchief held over the microphone). Many microphones these days have built-in wind guards. But, if possible , avoid recording in the wind.

40. Background noises sometimes isn't obvious to the human ear (which can be very selective about sound). But the microphone picks up everything within its "field". Background noise can add interest to a recording, but it should not distract the listener from what is being said.

41. Appropriate background noise (for example, the sound of the engine you're talking about) can provide the interview with added interest . But, whether the background is wanted or not, try to keep it at the same level (degree of loudness) otherwise you'll run into problems when editing later.

42. It may be better to record the interview separately from the sounds you want. Then you can mix them later in the studio when you are putting the programme together. Record the interview and the sound on separate tapes.

43. When you rocord the interview, let the tape recorder run silently for five or ten seconds. Do the same at the end of the interview. You will find this "atmosphere" useful when editing.

44. **Recording.** Know all about tape recorder so you don't have any problems when preparing for the recording. While you're discussing the interview, balance the voices of yourself and the interview. Place the microphone so the meter reading (level) is the same for both voices.

45. Remember some general points:
    (a) Your voice projection is likely to be better than that of your interview, so the microphone probably will be closer to him.
    (b) The less the microphone moves the better.
    (c) Hold the microphone firmly youself, do not let the interview grab it.

46. Always consider the possibility that you might need to edit:
    (a) keep the background noise constant,
    (b) don't talk over the interview, exert where absolutely necessary,
    (c) if you have to, re-record unsatisfactory questions and answers,

note on a piece of paper details relating to each recording made, don't rely on your memory.

(d) avoid using such words as "first" and "finally" (when editing you might want to chance the order of the question),

(e) avoid any reference to time such as "today" or "next week" (the interview may be programmed in two weeks time).

47. If the word happens and you are running out of tape, switch the machine to a slower speed.

48. Before you start the interview, give an identification. The identification should run like this: "identification. This is an interview with Mr. Zahir Hussain, Deputy Minister of Education. The interview is about the development of community schools. The interviewer is Ramesh. Record to Monday the eighth August. End of identification".

49. Editing the interview:

Good planning reduces the need for editing, which takes time. Make sure you've done everything possible to record the perfect interview. Then try to keep things to plan. But, of course, things rarely go just as you want them to.

50. Editing may be necessary to:

(a) make an item run for the right length of time,

(b) dull parts of the interview,

(c) remove faults, whether spoken or technical,

(d) improve the interview generally.

51. Always be careful in editing that you do not change the meaning of what is said.

52. When you edit the interview:

(a) know exactly what you wanted to do,

(b) note the first and last words of the pieces you want to take out,

(c) preferably, know the lengths of the cuts you want to make.

53. Plan your opening announcement so the edited interview will follow on from it naturally. Good editing should be clear, leave the important information untouched and sound natural. Editing must not leave out important material, it must not give the wrong emphasis.

54. If the listener hears an edit, he may notice more than bad technique. He may ask himself why the edit was made. What was left out? Why?

Quiz on "Techniques of Interviewing"

1. Why do we interview?

(a) To understand people better

(b) To obtain news or fresh information of public interest

(c) To be able to make friends

(d) To find out whether we are popular with people

2. Conducting an intelligent and interesting interview requires:

(a) Good voice and clear elucidation

(b) Skill and good judgement

(c) Politeness and friend lines

(d) Sense of humour

3. Which is the most effective keyword to start a question?

(a) Will (b) Is

(c) Why (d) Has

4. Indicate another effective keyword for beginning a question:

(a) Can (b) Do

(c) Should (d) How

5. A good interviewer has to be

(a) An expert talker

(b) A clever humorous

(c) A shy and timid person

(d) A courteous detective and expert listener

6. The essential requirement for good interviewing is:

(a) A very high level of education

(b) Firmness of character

(c) Friendliness

(d) A deep and abiding curiosity about people

7. Generally speaking, how long should an interview last?
   (a) 12 Minutes
   (b) 6 Minutes
   (c) Like a s skirt-long enough to cover the subject, short enough to be interesting
   (d) 3 to 4 minutes

8. What form should the interview take?
   (a) Fully-scripted
   (b) Half-scripted and half-unscripted
   (c) Only the first question is scripted
   (d) The first and last question are scripted

9. In order to get better response, what of these questions would you ask a job seeker at an employment agency?
   (a) Are you now unemployed?
   (b) "Are you looking for a job just now, or waiting for a while?"
   (c) I understand you have found it difficult to get job. Is it because you are too choosy?

10. Which among these four is the appropriate question?
    (a) "Tell me why you've decided to do this?"
    (b) "Is it true that you' ve come to conduct some management courses for RTM staff officers?"
    (c) "For what purpose and for how long will you be engaged in your survey work?"
    (d) "Have you been sent by your organisation to come to Malaysia?"

11. "Which among these is the best worded question?
    (a) "Did you find it hot?"
    (b) "What effect does the heat have on you ?"
    (c) "Do you find our climate much warmer than yours?"
    (d) "How do you like our weather ?"

12. When you want to express appreciation to the interviewee during the interview, what do you do ?

(a) Say "Well, its very clever of you ...."

(b) Say "Oh, that's really wonderful ...."

(c) Move your head in approval, smile silently in appreciation or show "thumbs up" sign.

(d) Give poke-faced look without revealing thoughts feelings.

13. Where would you place you major question for the sake of the listener?

(a) Bright at the beginning of the interview

(b) At the very end

(c) Somewhere at the half-way mark

(d) Immediately preceeding the final question

14. When the interviewee asks you a question, what must you do?

(a) Answer it in the normal way

(b) Ignore it and hope he wan't be annoyed

(c) Use the reverse question techniques

(d) Just giggle and hope for the best

15. During the test-recording, it is important

(a) to ask the actual questions that you have planned

(b) not to ask the actual question that you have planned

(c) to ask atleast one of the actual questions

(d) to ask atleast three of the actual questions

16. When recording an interview

(a) Your voice should be louder than the interviewe's voice

(b) The interviewee's voice should be much louder than yours

(c) The interviewee's voice should sound a little bit louder and slightly more prominent than your voice.

(d) Both voice levels should be of equal strength

17. Using a lot of vocal mannerisms in an interview

(a) helps to make the interview better

(b) adds a professional touch to the interview

(c) can irritate or distract the listner

(d) helps to make the interviewer sound intelligent

18. How would you handle a 'gasbag' interviewee?
    (a) Let him go on without interruption
    (b) Cut in appropriately when he takes a breath pause
    (c) Encourage him to divert from the topic
    (d) Show your disapproval with sarcastic remarks

19. An interviewer will be surprised how much interesting and useful information he can get out of the other person
    (a) by using a condenscending slavish approach
    (b) by using the mutual eye contact technique
    (c) by adopting an adamant attitude
    (d) by being extremely compromising.

20. How do you round up an interview? Which of these expressions is suitable?
    (a) "Well, I don't think there's many more to talk about ....."
    (b) "Unfortunately our time is up, so before I close 1 want to thank you ......"
    (c) "I wish you will have a pleasant stay in our country".
    (d) "Is there anything else you would like to say?"

□

11

CLASSROOM 2000 PLUS – A STUDY ON INTERACTIVE VIDEO TECHNOLOGY IN INDIA

Under the auspices of Indo-U.S. Sub-Commission, the project on Interactive Video Technology popularly known as Classroom 2000 Plus is a classic example of joint Indo-U.S collaboration to improve the quality of secondary education. U.S. experts on educational technology visited India and planned a series of meetings with their counterparts in the Ministry of Human Resource Development (HRD), Government of India and the Central Institute of Educational Technology (CIET), National Council of Educational Research and Training, an autonomous Institution of the Ministry of HRD. A well thought out plan was prepared to transact the selected difficult concepts in Mathematics and Physics for the students in five cities of India at a distance of hundreds of kilometers from each other.

Interactive video is an innovative tool of education in the learning systems and a beginning in this direction was made through the initiative taken in the early nineties by Indo-U.S. Sub-Commission. Television programmes were telecast live from 3rd to 7th May, 1993 after working out a well-designed strategy. Basic objective of the project was to use television with talk-back facility through telephone, computer and key pads.

Experts/teachers were the presenters in the studios and the students from various centres could interact with the experts/presenters through telephones, key pad-based computerized response system. Some of the inherent features of the project were:

(i) The interaction through direct telecast was confined to Kendriya Vidyalyas each in Mumbai, Kolkata, Hyderabad, Chennai, Ghaziabad and Nav Yug School, New Delhi.

(ii) The students could interact with the expert presenters through telephones, computerized key pads for quick feedback.

(iii) Active participation in the demonstration lessons was restricted to 65 students in the schools which were equipped with colour television, telephone, computer and interactive key pads.

(iv) Demonstrations/lectures were telecast live from the television studios of National Council of Educational Research and Training (NCERT), New Delhi to Doordarshan Studios through the microwave link, uplinking to satellite. During the live sessions, the presenter teacher raised questions for quick responses from the students. These responses were tabulated within seconds and enabled the presenter teacher to have an idea as to how many students have made the correct responses.

(v) Interactive power of computer and the television combines together the the potentials of many teaching-learning devices, destined to make an impact on the quality of education in enabling the learners to respond and play an active part in the transaction of instructional material allowing greater freedom to make teaching learning effective, interesting and stimulating.

As a part of the research design, the students were divided into three groups in each Centre, viz. the experimental group, control group I and control group II. There were total number of ten students in the experimental group who had been provided the telephone line and the key pads for raising questions and for interacting with the presenters which was an essential and salient feature of the project.

Control group I had also 10 students from the same class who had been provided with the facilities of viewing television presentation but without the telephone line and the key pads unlike their class mates in the experimental group. Control group II comprised of Vidyalayas which had been provided the facilities of viewing television but they were not aware of the provision of telephone lines and the key pads, provided to the students in the experimental groups. Evaluation of the project was entrusted to All India Association for Educational Technology, New Delhi. Prime objective of the project was to know the impact of interactive technology on the specific content areas in the teaching learning process, especially difficult concepts in Physics and Mathematics at the senior secondary school level. NCERT, through its evaluation team also conducted the study independently to know the impact of the project and the results of both the evaluation studies matched with each other and came out with the conclusion that there was a positive and significant difference in the achievement of comprehension in the subject areas of Physics and Mathematics among the experimental and control groups.

The capability to use key pads by the students was largely acquired as a result of interaction between the technical experts of U.S.A. and India. The experiment was of a short duration of five days but it took almost a year for planning and execution after mutual exchange of ideas and experiences which have opened new vistas of interactive technology as an accepted instructional innovation for the students and teachers on a vast scale.

The noble and innovative experiment of Classroom 2000 Plus has made a significant dent in the formulation of policies in education to cater to the needs of orientation of nearly 50 lakh school teachers of India as training can be imparted to 10,000 teachers in various centres which are provided with the facilities of dish antennas, telephone lines, computers and as a follow up of this project, teleconferencing programmes known as one-way video and two-way audio as a part of the "Special Orientation of Primary Teachers" Project of the Government of India, have been launched in various States of India, with uplink facilities provided by Indian Space Research Organisation, Indira Gandhi National Open University, National Institute for Open Schooling, and the NCERT. The project besides being exploratory and stimulating, also raises the curiosity of the learners, who find themselves in the realm of unfold experimental universe, turned into classroom for optimum gains.

India has a bigger challenge to achieve universalisation of Elementary Education and interative media through teleconferencing on a mass scale which can help in achieving the gigantic task of inculcating positive attitudes in the adults and young children towards learning. Research inputs in the system may perhaps be feasibly incorporated so that the advanced technologies could be employed for mutual exchange of experiences in the educational institutions and the student could venture, explore and visualize the concepts on important scientific facts and processes for easy comprehension which is a major objective of interactive video. The project is a source of motivation and has broken the monopoly of rigid curriculum by correlating materials, themes and final execution through observations, presentations and demonstrations rather than by providing mere explanations through written/spoken words. Students and the community could get the maximum benefit in the form of entertainment, enrichment and broaden their horizons.

The marriage of computer with television providing interactivity combines many teaching-learning devices with far-reaching impact on education, training, retraining of teachers on a vast scale. The system is economically viable and less costly with its wider coverage and minimal supervision. Development costs vary depending upon the size, level or degree of interactivity and production values. Major segments of the cost is involved in the preparation of appropriate design and in integrating videos with computer softwares and the rest of the cost is on the development of software and video production and administrative set up. Once the dish antenas are procured and set up at the centres where the teachers and learners are to assemble, instructions can be easily passed on through the studios uplinkings. The added advantage is that just in one programme of specific duration, orientation can be provided to a large number even upto 10,000 persons which is otherwise not possible in the traditional mode. Thus, the project on classroom 2,000 plus has opened enormous possibilities about its effectiveness in the teaching-learning process with many obvious benefits which have been the outcome of the collaboration of Indo-US Sub-Commission, on Education. These are effective and inexpensive alternatives to the linear method of supplementing television for better comprehension of difficult concepts of the curriculum and for providing orientation training to the teachers in order to update their knowledge and skills of teaching. The awareness and application of this technology may result in increasing creativity and innovation in education both in rural as well as urban population of India. The project was initiated by the NCERT and its evaluation was entrusted to All India Association for Educational Technology. The main finding of the study were that Video Interactive Technology has resulted in achieving higher cognitive levels. Through this project, it has been possible to explore and experiment satellite link telecast with the talk-back facilities such as telephone, student response through key pads and computerized feedback with significant impact on learning. It has also been established from the experiment that interactive technology as an instructional innovation would be easily acceptable to the teacher-facilitators and learners. It has the potentialities and feasibility of improving the instructions both at formal as well as non-formal levels. Learner in a distant mode is more independent and self-reliant as compared to be in the conventional mode. One-way video and two-way audio and now two-way video being harnassed in India on a regular basis, are mainly the outcome of the experiment on Interactive Video Technology initiated in May 1993.

Pacing

Generally, students and teachers found the pacing of TV lessons okay. But a few times it was reported to be rather fast, particularly in Mathmatics lessons. There were suggestions from quite a few sources that the pacing of lessons might be carefully worked out keeping in view the entry level knowledge of the average students about the topics. New and difficult concepts would demand greater effort at concept clarification through more number of visuals, and hence slower pacing. This implies feeding systematically collected feed-forward data into lesson planning.

Feasibility of the Project

That there is technical feasibility to use the demonstrated technology for interactive teaching at a distance has been clearly established by the experiment. To the question whether the technology system would be useful and relevant in Indian context, the answer seems to be a big YES. If interviews in the field, and if mail received from the students, teachers, educationists, media experts and others are any indication, the demonstration has created a widespread awareness and teachers would also gain from students' programmes by viewing expert presentation as models worth emulating.

Another option to use the technology could be for in-service teacher training. There is a huge backlog of unqualified and untrained teachers at all school levels. Frequent changes in the syllabus as knowledge expands, also demand that teachers must be kept abreast with not only the new concepts, but also the pedagogy of teaching these concepts. The technology can come in handy to meet with the problem of retraining a large number of teachers effectively in a short span of time. Most of the teacher co-ordinators when asked to choose between students' education and teacher training, preferred the latter. Six out of ten teachers co-ordinators said that if one were to prioritise, teacher training would be a better option.

Classroom Management

In the event of using the technology for supplementary teaching, the role of class teacher would change to interacting with the students to solve their problems, refer them to other resource materials, and giving them greater drill/practice. The teachers would need orientation and develop appreciation for their new role. They would also need training in placement of the TV at the right height and angle, and operation of the TV set interest about the potential of the system in improving the quality of education, increasing access and removing disparities in education at the secondary level.

There is, however, a limitation. The configuration information sub-system as available in the software supplied by the KET allows for only a limited number of the active participants at a time. It is possible to redesign the software to accommodate a larger student population via computer networking. But even with the existing software, it should not really prove to be a deterrent. The study has clearly shown that non-participating students found the technology nearly as useful and exciting as the participating students. The implications of the this finding in respect of scaling down of the Project are far reaching. It implies that supply of computer and telephone hardware to every viewing student may not be necessary. A few carefully selected participating schools could set a stage for all other students in schools or in homes in the country for effective learning. All they would need is the relevant equipment.

Options for Using the Technology

Non-uniformity of the syllabus in different regions (except for CBSE students) may pose a problem to extend the scope of the project for covering a larger and heterogenous student community. The options to use the system could be:

– to give tutorial lessons at certain periods as preparation for the final examination taking difficult topics/concepts in sciences/ mathematics.
– to give lessons as supplementary teaching to the classroom teaching throughout the year for strengthening and reinforcing the concepts in science/mathematics following the CBSE syllabus.
– In case of students learning by open education, the video-tapped lessons placed in study centres would serve as good source materials.

The Classroom 2000+ Project was supported by:

(i) The Ministry of Human Resource Development Govt. of India, for Project identification and funding. 2.24 million.

(ii) The Indɔ-US Sub Commission on Education and Culture for identifying the technology system for interactive distance teaching and project support.

(iii) The Kentucky Educational Television Network (KET) Laxington, USA for transfer of technology and training. For this purpose a team of the KET visited India in August 1992. The Indian team visited the KET in February 1993 for orientation. The KET also loaned the computer software and 100 pieces of key pads for use in the experimentation.

(iv) The United State Information Agency in India for arranging the supply of the KET hardware and software and project co-ordination.

(v) The Doordarshan for uplinking the live TV lessons to the Indian National Satellite and transmitting the TV lessons on national network and regional networks and for arranging advance publicity to the project through inserts.

(vi) The Computer Maintenance Corporation (CMC) for arranging the supply of the classroom computers at seven different locations and the main computer at the CIET along with modems and associated periphery, and maintaining them. They also manned and supervised key pad and computer operations in the participating schools and in the CIET.

(vii) The Kendriya Vidyalaya Sangathan (KVS) for deputing its five schools spread over different locations in the country to participate directly in the experiment. A New Delhi Municipal Corporation School, namely the Senior Navyug School, and an extension of this school set up in the CIET also actively participated. The KVS directed their other schools all over the country to view the TV lessons, and send comments to the CIET.

(viii) Numerous students/teachers all over the country who viewed the interactive TV lessons in their schools and homes.

The project was widely publicised through Doordarshan and newspapers to create awareness about it.

For the CIET, this was a new and exciting experience of handling live television lessons using fairly complicated system. Systems management and team work made the execution of the project successful.

The designing, structuring and presentation of the interactive lessons involved intense planning and work. The presentation of the lesson started with a discussion on the previous-day assignment work. After introducing the unit, the teacher then presented new concepts. After each concept, the teacher asked questions to test comprehension and application of the knowledge of the students, and provided clarification by giving the correct answer. Subject matter experts assisted the TV teachers in providing clarifications and expanding the concepts in reply to the questions raised by the participating students. The list of the names of the teachers/experts who contributed towards this effort is given in Appendix II.

The All India Association of Educational Technology was contracted to do an evaluation of the Project independently as an outside agency. At then the same time the CIET also evaluated the project. Ms. Jai Chandiram, the them Joint Director, CIET and the Project Co-ordinator provided able guidance at various stages of the study from setting out objectives, preparation of research tools to the presentation of the report.

At the instance of the CIET, the State Institutes of Educational Technology (SIETs) also collected data from some participating and some non-participating students/teachers which was used for the evaluation of the programe.

References

Bovy, Rl (1981) : Successful Instructional Methods, Cognitive Information Processing Approach; Educational Communication & Technology Journal, USA.

Chapman, D.W. and Carrier (1990) : Improving Educational Quality A Global Perceptive, West port et, green-wood press.

Evans C. (1983) : The Making of a Macro; A History of Computer, Oxford Press, London.

Hirschbul John. J (1992) : Multimedia : Why Invest? Interactive learning: International & press.

NCERT, New Delhi (1998) : Interactive Videos Technology, An Indian Experience: International Review of Education Journal.

Phutela RL (1996) : A Pilot Project on Internactive Video Technology for Karnataka state by NCERT.

SITE (1975) : Satallite Instructional Telesvision Experiment, Ministry of HRD (Min of Education) Govt. of india.

Sebastian G (1995) : Using Technology to prepare teachers, California, Corivan Press; USA

SRRI (1994) : Impact of Educational Telecast, Social and Rural Research Institute, New Delhi.

□

12

INFORMATION AND COMMUNICATION TECHNOLOGY AND MULTIMEDIA IN EDUCATION

Abstracts

Information and Communication Technology, (ICT) has revolutionalsed the education system all over the world. Initially, it was considered as an imported luxury from the West. Even the teachers/tutors believed that ICT does not contribute to the teaching-learning process. Today ICT, with the inherent power of interactivity, multimedia and with a provision of dynamic and flexible system of education, caters to the diverse needs of society. Transmission and broadcasting technologies, harnessed with audio, video and teleconferencing technologies and other inputs such as Edusat, Teleconferencing, Internet, etc. have made it possible to reach to a large segment of society for skill upgradation and life-long learning.

Through ICT initiatives, it is possible to achieve excellence in terms of quality of education and undertake Continuous and Comprehensive Evaluation (CCE) by exploring and utilizing the resources of education, available anywhere in the world.

The role of the various ICT initiatives with significant contribution to the teaching-learning processes has been briefly elaborated in the paper.

Information and Communication Technology (ICT) signifies the sets of technical tools and resources, both human and non-human which are

used to carry, to communicate, and to create, disseminate, store, retrieve and manage information systems. Such technologies include computers, their components and main functions; Broadcasting Technologies such as radio, television and telephony (both mobile and landline).

UNESCO (2002) defined the term Information and Communication Technology as the "form of technologies that are used to create, store, share or transmit and exchange information". Besides Computers and Computer Aided Instructions, it includes equipment and services associated with computers, radio, television, video, DVD, telephone, audio-video conferencing, internet and electronic mail. World Bank (2002) added another feature to the definition and made it more elaborate by supplementing further with the communication infrastructure part and referred to physical telecommunication systems and networks (cellar, broadcast, cable, satellite, postal, etc.) and the services that are utilized, viz. Internet, voice mail, radio and television. Information Technology when integrated with communication implies hardware and software of information collection, storage, processing, presentation and dissemination. The government declared (dated 10 January, 2012) a revised scheme on ICT to bridge the digital divide and to get 1.5 crores students acquainted with ICT system covering 1.08 lakh schools by providing dependable power supply and Internet connectivity. The revised ICT scheme aims at capacity building of more than one million teachers using ICT-based tools of teaching through induction and refresher training, both for formal schooling and for Open Distance Learning.

As early as 50 years ago, renowned scientist, Dr. Vikram A. Sarabhai had visualized the use of Satellite Broadcasting to reach out to the rural and backward areas of the country for social transmission. He was of the firm belief that the satellites were the tools for carrying information and thereby education to the masses. It is a fact that Dr. Sarabhai had laid the foundations information and Communication Technology (ICT) in India as early as in seventies which later culminated into various experiments such as Satellite Instructional Television Experiment (SITE) and other important ventures, exclusively for education.

Major ICT Initiatives in Education

After the launch of Satellite Instructional Television Experiment (SITE) in 1975-76, another systematic and large-scale effort to run an education programme with ICT was the Indian National Satellite (INSAT) in 1980, popularly known as INSAT for Education which was initially made available for school education. Simultaneously for higher education, University Grants Commission (UGC) Country Wide Classroom Project, was launched in collaboration with Doordarshan.

Educational Technology Division in the Ministry of Human Resource Development was set up along with the Central Institute of Educational Technology (CIET) in the National Council of Educational Research and Training (NCERT) and the State Institutes of Educational Technology (SIETs) in the States. The main task entrusted to the CIET, and the SIETs was confined to the production of educational television and radio programmes, imparting training to the personnel and researchers in media. All India Radio and Doordarshan were chosen as the carriers of the broadcasts/telecasts. Television and radio sets were supplied to the schools to make use of broadcasts/telecasts.

Computer Literacy and Studies in Schools (CLASS) was the project introduced in 1984-85 and a part of the project, 12000 computers were distributed to the schools. The scheme discontinued in the 9th Five Year Plan but a revised scheme on Computer launched later in 2001-02.

National Task Force on Information Technology and Software Development was constituted by the Government of India in 1998 which made a significant recommendation regarding the introduction of IT in Education. The specific recommendation made by the Task Force was to provide computers to all the educational institutions at the Secondary/ Senior Secondary level. Educational Technology and the 'CLASS' schemes were modified and a new scheme known "ICT in Schools" was formed to meet the educational challenges and needs to collaborate, share and revitalize learning through alternative modes.

IT Policy

Many states have computer education component built-in as part of the IT policy. The Act provides legal recognition for transactions by means of electronic communication involving the use of alternatives to paper-based methods of communication and storage of information and to facilitate and maintain documents electronically. As a part of Computer Aided Learning (CAL), provision of Mobile Computer Laboratory is the other initiative, taken by the State Governments at the district level. Four Computers are fitted in the van with projector and a screen. The van visits the schools which do not have computers in their schools and screen the programmes.

Instruments and Applications of ICT

ICT is indispensable today and is being integrated with the teaching-learning practices as it allows flexibility for experimentation and innovations with ICT inputs so that it becomes easier to understand and comprehend effectively. For improving the quality of education and transaction of content, ICT initiatives are required to be weaved and integrated with the system. These components include multimedia, animation and other computer-aided instructions which are now being taken up as preferred choice of career options by the increasing number of students. There is also a great demand for the students who have completed these courses and are geared for production of programmes in multimedia.

In order to improve the quality of education, it is considered essential to make the system efficient in terms of access and delivery mechanism through the instruments of IT by integrating it with the curriculum which not only enhances the quality and reach but also makes the process interactive. Simultaneous interaction tantamounts to the virtual classroom environment lively and joyful with the help of latest technologies. Today we cannot think of education without ICT inputs. Dr. A.K. Bakshi, former Director, Institute of Life Long Learning, University of Delhi elaborated (article published in TOI dated 1 June 2009) that ICT has the unique distinction of comprehending the difficult concepts with ease as ICT serves as an agent for a favourable change and empowers the teachers to find solutions to the problems, inherent in the teaching-learning process. ICT initiatives also enable the teachers and the learners to think creatively and enrich their experiences as these technologies are the most powerful tools for problem-solving and helpful in conceptual development and creative thinking. Computer technology provides access to data including information storage, retrieval and collection of data, collaborate with others via networks, promotes research and related activities which otherwise cannot be carried out with ease.

MULTIMEDIA EDUCATION

Multimedia, an important component of ICT, can be described as two or more media combined to provide information about a subject or concept with the help of computer. The elements of multimedia are text, drawings, graphs, photographs, film, video, wireless, audio, animation, web, etc. Multimedia denotes the combination of several media to transport information in several forms from one point to another. Many institutions are offering courses in multimedia which include print media, animation, web designing and computer disk authoring, etc. Multimedia has the potentials to create visual lessons for the targeted learners. With the interactive power of computer, it can make a major impact on education, training, information services and entertainment. It is one of the most rapidly challenging and enriching areas of education in the world today which offers the teachers and the learners, access to the material as never before as it can deliver large amount of information in many ways which are manageable, accessible and immensely useful.

Multimedia is an offshoot of Computer Technology which is one of the most innovative techniques used by educationists throughout the world. This technology made its headway in India in mid-seventies. Initially, there was a feeling among the people that the multimedia being an imported luxury from the West, did not contribute to the teaching-learning process. But with the passage of time, it is now fully established that multimedia-based learning strategy is of utmost benefit to the students, teachers and educators, not only in enhancing the academic achievement but also in making learning environment, joyful and enriching. These new technologies offer access to materials as never before. The integration of multimedia programme with the content facilitates learning with ease.

Multimedia is defined as a system which exploits the computer to combine text, graphics, animation, audio, and video into a single synchronised production or presentation. Under this definition, CD ROMs, Internet, pen drive and films are multimedia delivery mediums. Planning, storyboarding, editing and authoring are the steps of development of multimedia. The main focus in this definition is the capability of the computer to exploit hardware and software to integrate different elements of the multimedia. These elements may be developed independently by various media sources into a multimedia user interface or presentation.

Multimedia

Writers have defined in many ways such as:

- A combination of multiple media types, including text, graphics, animation, audio and video is called Multimedia.
- The use of several media, such as movies, slides, music, and lighting in combination normally for the purpose of education or entertainment.

- Computer-controlled presentations combining three or more of the following elements: text, graphics, animation, full-motion images, still video images, and sound.
- Software programs that combine text and graphics with sound, video, and animation. A multimedia PC contains the hardware to support these capabilities.
- A term used to describe a range of products that have some audio and/or visual basis; for example, encyclopaedia programs are called "multimedia" besides animation, both 2-D and 3-D.
- Systems "that support the interactive use of text, audio, still images, video, and graphics.
- Multimedia is the integration of multiple forms of media. This includes text, graphics, audio, video, etc.

It is evident from the definitions of that multimedia encompasses a wide spectrum of applications and technology. Anyone or more of the following media and/or a combination of audio, text, graphics, animation and video is generally employed in all multimedia projects in the field of education.

Elements of Multimedia

Text, audio, video, animation and graphics are the elements of the multimedia.

Text-Text is an important element of media. Text is used in multimedia for the different purposes such as

- Title texts
- Body texts
- Menu
- Miscellaneous texts

Audio plays a vital role in the making of a multimedia. In multimedia, audio is put in the form of

- Natural sounds
- Music
- Dialogues
- Narrations

While developing multimedia, audio recording is a serious business and it needs great effort and expertise.

Video is made up of a series of frames of slightly varied images which when shown in rapid succession gives the impression of movement. A video clip is a sequence of images that are displayed rapidly to give the impression of movement. To give smooth motion, PC needs to display over 25 frames per second-each frame has separate image so even a short video clip takes up huge amount of space on disk.

Animation literally means to bring something to life. A computer-based animation is an animation performed by a computer using graphical tools to provide visual effects. It is yet another feature of multimedia capabilities.

Two-Dimensional (2-D) Animation is the most common type today, such as cartoons. However, 3-D Animation has mostly been confined to the engineering field like Computer-Aided Design (CAD). As 3-D Animation technology matures and becomes more competitive, this feature will also get into applications like on-line tutorials, simulations and virtual classrooms.

Graphies playa major role in any multimedia application. All formats of graphics can be presented. Jresented in a multimedia. An image represents a still picture in digital form by using \bits to specify the colour of each of the many pixels. An image is spatial representation of an object, a two-dimensional or three-dimensional scene or another image. It can be real or virtual. An image is a still photograph used for adding visual effect to multimedia. In computer vision, an image is usually a recorded image such as video image or a picture. In computer graphics, an image is always digital in nature.

TYPES OF MULTIMEDIA

The multimedia programmes are mainly of two types:

- Linear
- Non-Linear

(A) Linear- Early multimedia was linear in nature. In linear multimedia, the end user receive a programmes, which plays a sequence of sound, video and images without any control over the presentations content. So linear media is general in nature.

(B) Non-Linear- In contrast to linear, if the programme lets the user control the sequence by selecting different options, it is called Interactive Multimedia or Non-linear multimedia.

Interactive and Non-Interactive Multimedia:

A clear distinction can be made between 'interactive' multimedia and 'non-interactive' multimedia on the basis of interactivity level. Interactivity relates to communication between the multimedia system and its user, i.e. it requires input from its audience. Interactive media may also be accessed to various sequences by the user, where as non-interactive multimedia tends to be linear in sequence. Interactive multimedia has been called a "hybrid technology". It combines the storage and retrieval capabilities of computer database technology with advanced tools for viewing and manipulating these materials. Multimedia has a lot of different connotations, and definitions vary depending on the context. In the context of school education, interactive multimedia may be defined as any package of materials that includes some combination of texts, graphics, still images, animation, video, and audio. These materials are packaged, integrated and linked together in such a way that offers and analyses indexing features with capacity to create good teaching-learning environment.

Multimedia is capable of delivering large amount of material in multiple forms in the an integrated environment that allows the students to have the wonderful reading, listening and viewing experiences by allowing users to control the sequence and pacing of the materials. Multimedia packages facilitate greater individualization in learning. Multimedia allows students to proceed at their own pace in a tailored learning environment. Furthermore, multimedia can be a powerful learning and teaching tool because it engages multiple senses. Students learning multimedia are reading, seeing, hearing, and actively participating in the class.

"As humans, we seem hard-wired for the multiple inputs. We remember only about 10% of what we read, 20% if we hear it, 30% if we can see visuals related to what we're hearing, 50% if we watch someone do something while explaining it, but almost 90%, if we do the job ourselves-if only as a simulation. In other words, interactive Multimedia-properly developed and properly implemented-could revolutionize education." (Menn,1993)

The use of Multimedia for education is increasing day by day both in formal and non-formal sectors, i.e. illustrated stories to support the language teaching, demonstration of the experiments or to prepare the animated pictures to explain the concepts in the Mathematics/ Environmental Sciences and other subjects. Multimedia packages can enrich the experiences of the children and help the teachers to enrich the text and study materials.

Now a days, multimedia programmes are developed on various theme. The development of multimedia packages involves listing of the concepts/ sub-concept, programme briefs and content outlines. Planning for the pre-production includes preparation of a storyboard, development of the script, systematic collection, the creation of the graphics programming with the sound and the visual recordings on the computer and lastly testing and dissemination with the target groups. Occasionally, television camera shots are also added to the computer graphics resulting into a virtual marriage of the television with the computer for better results. All media programmes whether audio, video or computer aided generally originate from a given theme of a topic which is the basic step in planning and production. The themes or ideas are processed and refined thoroughly and expanded further in the form of the programme outline or programme brief.

Today, multimedia is considered as the seamless digital integration of text, graphics, animation, audio, still images and motion video in a way that provides wonderful experience to the user. The evolution of multimedia is a story of the emergence and convergence of the technologies.

THE EVOLUTION OF MULTIMEDIA

Evolution of multimedia can be woven around five themes developed over a time line-visionaries, text processing and software, audio and telecommunication, computers, video and animation.

Visionaries-Innovations of the outstanding thinkers had a direct impact on the explosion of the technological age. So the ingenious idea of the programmable computer can be traced back to the innovations of visionaries.

Text, Processing and Software-Inventions and innovations that spawned the development of software enabling computers to move from mathematical processing to technology, which creates and delivers multimedia.

Computers-From academic and corporate worlds, we can trace computer development from gigantic, nosy, bulky dinosaur computers to the role of the sleek, handy and efficient desktop personal computer and laptop of today.

Audio and telecommunication-From the telegraph signal to cellular telephones and the development from analog signal to digital transmission of voice

Video and Animation-From manually manipulated negative film and hand drawn sketches, video and animation developed to sophisticate digital creation and rendering of motion.

The multimedia revolution has changed for ever; what computers can do for us by giving those new ways to present information and act as powerful source of information and communication.

The simplicity and power of multimedia enriches teacher's creativity and leads to multi-sensory student learning. It is also a whole lot of fun besides contributing to the teaching-learning process immensely.

The development and use of multimedia has transformed the world of education by creating a huge impact on the learners as well as on the teachers.

Internet- known as network ICT-based content resources are being developed for optimum use. Internet is one such resource which is fast spreading even in remotest areas of the country. Due to various initiatives taken by the Government and the corporate sector, Internet Technology connects computers all over the world making every computer accessible to every other computer. We can connect our computer to the network as and when we want and have access to the computer to meet our needs and requirements. We can put into place excellent teaching-learning resources in the network to pool the required resources which could be in the form of pictures, video, clippings, visuals, animations, lesson plans and related activities in an interactive way. Messages can be sent through electronic mail without any loss of time. We can also chat with the teachers and fellow learners for discussions and seek guidance for mutual benefit. In a way, the technology is helping individuals to learn independently by using Internet resources. Internet access has changed the way of our lives.

It has brought sea changes in the education practices. Many online education websites have evolved to help the learners. Counseling for learners in assessment, performance analysis and guidelines are being provided on the Internet who are aspiring to take up engineering, medicine or other professions. This includes the guidance to the students on how to prepare for various examinations. On-line education for admission and on-demand examination especially for Open Distance Learners are gaining popularity because of increasing distances, lack of time and financial constraints, enabling the teachers to bring creativity and give the learners an opportunity to prove their worth independently by improving their instructional skills through Internet. They can take full advantage of the up-to-date information which is otherwise not available in the text materials. Large number of students and researchers make use of Internet for e-mail, course materials, research and special areas of education. We can safely say that the use of Internet in Education is firmly established.

Educational Radio/Television and ICT

With the advent of digital technology as a fringe to the ICT, there is a virtual revolution in the restructuring of the education system in our country. Now we are in a digital age with reality television shows and breaking news reports. Films are now being produced in a digital format which are closer to reality. Smaller pocket-sized cameras are available which not only bring authenticity to the visuals but are superior for quality productions. The digital medium has a major influence on the future of educational programmes. Digital format is most effective, economical and flexible. It provides scope for non-linear editing and saves lot of time and energy for efficient and fine production of programmes. LCD projectors can preview and project on programmed CD. The process of production is cheapest and easy.

Studies have been conducted on the use of educational television/ audio-radio programmes, at various levels which establish the effectiveness of the educational radio and television. The interactive mode has been found to be more effective than the talk-back mode. It is established that educational radio/educational television has been credibly used to achieve the desired objectives. It is also revealed that educational radio/educational television programmes are highly effective if these are in interactive mode. A marriage between the computer and the television is the optimum choice to bring interactivity in the programmes. Various strategies can be gainfully worked out so that there is no distortion.

The nature of ETV programmes is fast changing to digital mode on computers or to digital projection. The educational or even edutainment programmes are now increasingly available on disks or CDs. The traditional film laboratories are now facing big crisis. It is evident that there is an end, of the educational film laboratories. It is evident that there is an end of the educational films. The 21st century is virtually the digital century for film educational programmes.

- Digital television and audio broadcast technologies have changed the nature of educational television and radio broadcasting, resulting into the transformation of the education system. There is a digital convergence of all the media. There is a radio-on-demand service, developed by All India Radio website. When one dials its code number X, it is forwarded to the processor and scheduling computer correlated to digital audio, stores it. The song gets selected and queued. When you register, the voice interactive system tells you the exact time when it will be played.

- Use of Satellite Communication and Information Technology in the teaching-learning process and education of the teachers is a virtual reality today. Internet and knowledge-based resources have provided immense possibilities to improve the classroom processes and in-service education of the teachers once the interactive technology is set up. The training cost using this mode is less to that of the traditional face-to-face training methodology. This strategy can substantially reduce training loss at successive levels. Interactive technology, therefore, opens up possibilities for creative use of resources. The audio/teleconferencing approach to education uses two-way audio and one-way video tapes/CDs computer system, telephones and radio and television broadcasts. The interactivity between the teachers/learners and experts is coordinated by an anchor person. Telephone Straight Trunk Dialing (STD) is used to ask questions to the expert panelists. Their answers are transmitted live from TV/audio studios which have an uplink with the transponder on INSAT Satellite operated by Indian Space Research Organisation (ISRO). This technology has opened up possibilities to provide training/orientation to the large group of teachers/learners and to offer distance learning opportunities on a mass scale. In a traditional type of training/orientation face-to-face programme, a maximum number of trainees could the 50 or so to give new innovations but in a teleconferencing mode even the number of persons participants could be more than 10,000 in one go. Besides being economical, instructions in the teleconferencing could be passed on directly from the resource persons to the participants whereas in the cascade mode, such instructions move from experts key persons to resource persons to participants, resulting into the huge transmission loss between the stake holders.

Education Satellite (EDUSAT)

The Indian Space Research Organisation (ISRO) launched EDUSAT on 20th Sept. 2004, enabling the use of multi channels devoted solely for educational activities as it was revealed that only a small fraction of satellite capacity was being made available for educational purposes. This reflects our commitment to use space technology for national development especially to serve the people in the rural and backward areas of the country. Each State Education Department was asked to make use of the new technology and seek help and technical support from ISRO and the Union Ministry of Human Resource Development (MHRD) for Higher Education, Consortium for Educational Communications (CEC) of the University Grant Commission (UGC), for Distance Education Programmes-Indira Gandhi National Open University (IGNOU) and the National Institute of Open Schooling, for Technical Education-All India Council for Technical Education and IITs for School Education programmes-Central Institute of Educational Technology (CIET), NCERT were entrusted with the responsibility for the development, production and transmission of programmes for the target groups. The work started at snail's pace and it can be safely stated that the programme could not achieve the objectives, specified for this project due to various reasons – the most important of them being the coordination between the stake holders, their own priorities and the financial constraints.

E-learning

Although E-learning is the outcome of computer and its applications, it is reckoned as a separate entity in view of its strategic importance it has gained in recent times. ICT-based virtual classrooms are a reality today in the open distance mode of learning. TV and radio bradcasting has helped in removing the barriers of space and resources.

Using amalgamation of technology and delivery mechanism with interactive learning, popularly known as E-learning provide opportunities for self-paced learning with the lifelong learning process. E-learning enables to reach learners all over the world which helps to experience other cultures and embrace them with logic. It also enables them to evaluate the effectiveness of training, reduced cost of training, simple, interesting and easy ways to comprehend in less time. Moreover, the content of E-learning is planned for presentation step by step covering interaction, explanation of concepts, practices, followed by research and evaluation and hence has the potentials of providing the right type of education and information to the people at appropriate time and place.

ICT and Vocational Education

In view of the special significance of Vocational Education in India, the role of Information and Communication Technology and its integration with Vocational Education is very significant. With the ICT inputs, there is an increasing focus on the educational reforms to modernize the system and strengthen it further to make it job oriented through the well-planned Curriculum on Vocational Education. It is to be ensured that technology-based skills for applications on the life long learners are practiced so that the learners achieve proficiency and perfection. Tie-ups with the establishments and industries specialized with the various aspects of ICT are to be integrated with educational institutions imparting education at various levels. Here the potentialities of ICT applications need to be linked with the text materials and supplemented with technology-based infrastructure and inputs. Vocational streams involve lot of practical experiments which cannot be conducted through the text materials. The practical aspect could be provided through E-labs with the help of calculations required for conducting particular practical in order to bring clarity of the results achieved from such experiments. The basic clarities shall be imbibed throughout the lives of the learners in the further professions of their choice. These E-labs can be accessed through the Internet.

Many job-oriented courses have been introduced in ICT by linking these courses with the need of ICT-enabled industries/establishments for example Accounting, Office Automation, Tailoring, Plumbing, Agriculture, Data Handling, Data Processing, Desktop Publishing, Music and Audio-Video, etc. This also includes courses on Cyber Security.

The learners have been provided a wide range of choices, catering to a variety of job options. The courses are in conformity with the National Vocational Education Qualifications Framework (NVEQF). There is a provision for changes and revision in order to maintain relevancy to the changed circumstances and requirements of the job market and the ever going trends. These courses are offered by integrating the technology in order to enable the learners to solve many problems by providing them skill-oriented training. Vocational Education Curriculum when combined with technology of competency-based concepts enables the learners to acquire multi-skill proficiencies to make it a life long education.

ICT for the Learners with Special Needs

ICT is a boom for the learners with special needs to receive relevant education and to make them self-reliant and self-sufficient. For the visually impaired audio tapes with relevant content materials can be very helpful. Such tapes have been devised by the open distance learning centres institutions on pet animals and birds. With the support of stuffed animals and birds along-with the relevant audio which the targeted learners can listen while touching the stuffed animals and birds, can know the characteristics of the animals and birds. Such inexpensive technological devices can foster creatively ICT is ushering in a revolution for the open distance learners with the help of practical and innovative technological devices through long distance teleconferencing, E-learning with special apparatus and instruments which are very user friendly for the differently abled to which they can easily access to improve the quality of education, Ministry of Human Resource Development. Deptt. of Education, Govt. of India has come out with a document on National Policy on ICT for school education to devise and sustain ICT-enabled activities and processes for promoting universal, equitable open and free access to a state-of-the-art ICT and ICT-enabled tools and resources to all the learners.

ICT stands for the relevant education that focuses on the development of employability skills in order to reach to the far-flung areas, covering both the backward urban/rural and the under-privileged sections of the society. Technology has come to play a key role to deliver the self-paced education through its delivery mode in making learning on "anytime anywhere" basis. If the use of ICT becomes a art of the pedagogy itself, teaching learning not only can be interesting and effective but more creative and relevant to their emerging needs as the learners shall be better prepared for tomorrow. Many hazardous and unsafe experiments can be demonstrated with the help of sophisticated apparatus and instruments of technology using digital media and computer-aided instructions along with the development and dissemination of audio- radio programmes to support and supplement the text materials.

To make the process of teaching learning effective is to a large extent the outcome of ICT which has provided a golden opportunity to the learners, enabling them to acquire knowledge and skills and revolutionalising their lives.

□

13
EDUCATIONAL TECHNOLOGY AND RESEARCH

The products and prototypes in education are the outcome of the use and application of systematic and scientific research methods. Educational Technology is a systematic way of designing, devising, and carrying out the various processes of learning and teaching in terms of specific objectives which are based on research to bring about effective and meaningful communication. Research according to dictionary meaning denotes investigation or enquiry to search for new facts in any branch of knowledge and to find out meaningful answers to such questions about the events by applying scientific methods of study.

So the term 'research' is a systematic and continuous process which seeks to integrate in a systematic way for verification of generalizations, based upon the identification of problems, statement and defination of such a problem or problems by formulating the hypotheses through deductive and inductive reasoning, observation and testing. This includes collection, complication, analysis of data and drawing conclusions. Therefore research mainly implies the solution of a problem through cause and effect relationship.

Types of Research

In research, we use various methods to achieve many purposes for collection of required information for application in various disciplines. Research is mainly classified under the following categories.

(a) Basic Research: The purpose of this type of research is to generate new facts or theory. This is also termed as theoretical or pure research.

(b) Applied Research: Implies application of theoretical concepts into the practical field of education by identifying the problems and finding solutions through the application of research methods.

(c) Action Research: Aims at the immediate application of theory with its emphasis on the solution of problems on a systematic basis which the researchers are facing in their real life situations. The objectives of this type of research is not only diagnostic but remedial also.

There are many problems in the educational institutions which the tutors/teachers might be facing in their day-to-day instruction but these problems are either ignored or no scientific observation is made to solve such problems, which are not visible with the result that this classroom process and practices continue to suffer.

There are various methods of research but which method is to be used in Educational Technology for better comprehension of the process of educational technology with special reference to mass media, is a complex question. The research involves communicators, educationalists to know which material and method of instruction would be most effective for a specific target group of learners. We have an easy access to many media-graphics teaching aids, electronic media such as TV, radio and other projected and non-projected aids and one or a combination of various types can be used after testing their effectiveness.

The quantative methods in education involving description as well as statistical analysis are used for the preparation of comprehensive research proposals including research design, viz. objectives, hypothesis, preparation of tools, compilation of data, its analysis and interpretation and the research report, etc., specifying the procedure and methods for doing the above-mentioned tasks.

Research in Educational Technology includes the study of human beings and infrastructure for education which takes into account the psychology, sociology and morality aspects; the process of teaching-learning of the subjects of study. In an era of communication with modern technologies, being harnessed in Education, for revitalising and improving the quality of education the role of research in Educational Technology has increased immensely. Factors affecting the performance of teachers with varying communication skills can be taken up as an area of research which may include the use of traditional graphics aids versus modern technologies and also the equilibrium between the two, keeping in view the availability, feasibility, financial implications and the outcomes in terms of achievement of each. How far computer aided instructions could help to solve the complex problems of content areas which encounter lot of difficulties to find equipment and infrastructure in rural/backward areas.

Pre-production research also termed as formative research aims at assisting programe production having direct relevance to the learner's development of audience profile, their need assessment, programme briefs, draft script, identification of locale, selection of presenters/experts are part and parcel of pre-production programme on TV/radio/computer research.

Product Research includes production, editing of programme, preview for quality and content assessment and its effectiveness for programme series. This also involves, pretesting of the prototypes and testing with the target audience.

Post Testing Research is also stated as Summative Evaluation to know the impact of the programmes both qualitative and commulative in nature. With the emergence of advanced and modern technologies, large number of research studies have been taken up recently in the various aspects of Educational Technology. Some of the studies are the use and impact of multimedia in the teaching of English, social sciences and the application of animation techniques for conducting experiments in the study of pure sciences. UNESCO sponsored case study on the Low-Cost/Appropriate Educational Material and Equipment in India was conducted by the National Council of Educational Research and Training, New Delhi in the eighties of the last century. Similarly, studies on the impact of educational television programs on specific content areas by the Development Educational and Communication Unit of Indian Space Research Organisation (ISRO), institutions like NCERT, UGC and State Institutes of Educational Technologies, etc. have been taken up from time to time. Tele-conferencing and impact of instructional Satellite launched by the Govt. of India in 1982 has been subtle and wide spread.

Research Design for various Aspects of Educational Technology

A researcher intends to fulfill the objectives of a proposed study in order to find solution to the problems, identified by him/her. Research design is an important instrument to develop research questions and hypotheses. An erroneous design can do great harm to the research proposal and may bring in significant result to the entire proposal. The design is a major step to establish relationships between two or more variables. The design also aims to demonstrate that the results are true in the real world if all the steps are followed as per the guidelines laid down in the research design.

Experiment research design allows the researcher to have a control on the independent variables and also on the environment. This design involves two groups and two variables; independent as well as dependent. The groups are control group and experimental group. There is no treatment for control group but in the experimental group the treatment is applied to compare the performance of the two groups. This is termed as pre-test and the post-test designs.

Keith F. Punch in his book *Introduction to Research Methods* (Sage Publications, N. Delhi, 2009) substituted the terms cause and effect which are the common terms used in research. The term 'cause' is applicable to quantitative research whereas the 'Effect' is used for qualitative research. We may explain these terms as below:

Cause	**Effect**
Independent Variables	Dependent variables
Treatment Variables	Outcome Variables
Pre-dictor Variables	Criteria Variables
Antecedents Determinants	Consequences

Depending upon the varying abilities of the learners it is evident that some individuals need verbal and graphic information and the supporting visual textual material. Research is also likely to influence to a great extent on the choice of a topic or identification of the problem.

Recent trends in Educational Technology have brought into the emergence of communication. Research among the media person, teachers and the learners and the persons trained in various aspects of research are able to go in search for scientific knowledge in a systematic manner. It is the scientific study of the behavior of human beings which requires primary quantitative information such as the media and the content of the message. This falls into the category of qualitative research which is difficult to measure the outcomes of such a research study. The majority of communication Research is related to Educational Technology. Hence, audience research becomes very significant. It is also very important to find out as to how the listeners/viewers perceive the messages and what are the barriers of communication. The local social or cultural context requires substantial modifications in research procedures to find out new ways of getting information, sampling and seeking responses through the specially designed tools/questionnaires rather than following the standard research procedures.

If the problems are social and moral in nature as compared to economic sphere, the degree of influence would vary. Modern methods of teaching and learning are being operated even without the use of visual material which are more effective by the intelligent researchers. It is also directly related to the stage of development of the communication process where the importance of logical presentation of the content diminishes due to the use of two-way process of communication.

As a part of one of the research tools, a sample questionnaire for Education Satellite known as Edusat Project meant for institutions producing Educational Television programs was developed which is appended at the conclusion of this chapter.

Research Report

Research report forms the hub of the research project and is central to the researcher objective of creating a basis of scientific knowledge for future use modification, if any use and dissemination of the research findings after covering each component of the research design during the process of investigation, preparation of hypotheses, tools, compilation of data, its analysis and final observations forms the basis. The researcher has to be unbiased and the observations are empirical. The questions which are to be kept in mind are:

(a) Are the hypotheses, if any, general, empirical and clearly defined in the research design?

(b) Are the dependent and in-dependent variable identifiable?

(c) Are the tools for data collection and complication measurable, quantifiable and observable?

(d) What is the type of language used, if any?

(e) Are the statistical methods used in the research appropriate?

(f) Whether the research findings specified and presented with conclusion drawn with clarity to find solution to the problem listed in the research design?

(g) Does it provide further scope of expansion of research study to solve-related problems with addition mrlification, if any?

The above questions need to be considered in the research study comprehensively. There are certain popular terms used in the research proposals which are listed in the concluding pages of this chapter. These terms would be useful in understanding the technical terms easily for explaining the complex problems faced by the researchers.

Sample questionnaire seeking details on the Educational Television/ audio-video programmes produced/acquired by the production centers

1. Name of the Organization: ____________

   (a) Complete Address: ____________

   ____

   Pin code no.: ____________

   b) i) Telephone number with station code: ____________

   ii) Mobile No. if any: ____________

   iii) Fax No. with station code: ____________

   c) E-mail: ____________

2. Date and year when established: ____________

3. Name of the controlling organization ____________
   with complete address ____________
   Pin Code No.: ____________

4. Total number of ETV programmes ____________
   produced yearwise since the inception of your ____________
   institue to date ____________

   (Please attach the list of programmes ____________
   along with CD indicating the target ____________
   audience, duration, synopsis and ____________
   language of each programme ____________

5. Total number of programmes produced ____________
   by your institute which have been ____________
   scheduled for telecast through T.V. Tele conferencing or ____________
   distributed to the learners on line CD each separately ____________
   (Mentisn year wise)

6. Total number of ETV/Audio Radio programmes produced by your institute which have not been telecast/broadcast (please specify reasons) ________

7. Total number of audio-radio programmes produced by your institute (year wise) Please attach the list alongwith CD indicating the target audience, duration, synopsesandlanguageofeach) ________

8. Please specify details of the members of the staff in your institute:
   (a) Total strength ________
   (b) Number of producers with pay scale ________
   (c) Number of production assistants ________
   (d) Number of scriptwriters with pay scale ________
   (e) Number of engineers with pay scale ________
   (f) Number of editors with pay scale ________
   (g) Number of Floor Assistants/Managers with pay scales ________
   (h) Number of graphicj computer artist with pay scale ________
   (i) Any other category ________

9. Average number of ETV and audio-radio programmes produced by each producer per year ________

10. Details of technical facilities/equipments ________
    (a) Number of video studios ________
    (b) Number of audio studios ________
    (c) Number of electronics cameras in studio with specifications — betacam/digital programmes ________
    (d) Number of E.N.G. Cameras ________
    (e) Editing Units ________
        (i) Linear Editing (Betacam U matic/DVS etc.) ________
        (ii) Cut to cut ________
        (iii) AB roll ________
        (iv) Non Linear Editing (NLE) ________
        (please give details of hardware and software)
        (v) Computer Animation ________
    (f) Lighting equipment with details ________
    (g) Recording Equipment for Audio programmes or any other digital ________

recording facilities if available such as ____________
Nagra etc. (please specify) ____________

(h) A.C. Plant with present status whether ____________
functioning satisfactionaly (please specify) ____________

(i) Any other facility available for production ____________
acquisition such as language dubbing ____________
etc. (please specify) ____________

(11) Number of programmes produced on turn key basis outsourced (please attach the list indicating the titles, duration etc.)

(i) Average cost of production of the outsourced programmes for 1/2 hours duration.

(ii) Average cost of production of inhouse programmes for 1/2 hours duration.

(12) (a) Whether the audio/video library has been computerized.

(b) Whether AV tapes digitized or not (please indicate its present position) ____________

(c) Number of programmes stored in tape formats

(i) Audio ____________

(ii) Video ____________

(d) Number of programmes transferred on CDs/DVDs ____________

(13) What broad aspects are kept in view while taking up the audio video programme with special reference to the following:

(a) Topic and broad relationship with syllabus, ____________
content and enrichment ____________

(b) Programme objectives, outcomes and level ____________
appropriate to the target audience ____________

(c) Script and treatment: Format using ____________
participatory techniques, pacing etc. ____________

(d) Production values: A V appeal, music, ____________
sound effects/animation, camera and ____________
lighting work ____________

(e) Technical quality and testing, sampling ____________
techniques in the case of programmes ____________
produced in series mode and "their" ____________

suitability from one to another. Quality of graphics, computer animation used. ______

(f) Interaction of producers with subject experts, script writers and the camera persons (Howfrequent) ______

(14) Has smoking/drinking been depicted in any E.TV programme. Please specify the title ______

(15) Comment on the optimum utilization of facilities with special reference to the following:

(a) Knowledge about the latest equipment for cost effective production/uplinking /EduSat (Please tick appropriately) Adequate Inadequate

(b) Planning for media strategies for use in EduSat/Teleconferencing (Please tick appropriately) Adequate Inadequate

(c) Use of emerging technologies for Inadequate formal as well non formal sections; Adequate Inadequate

(d) Assessing the future technical information in terms of Equipment planning and procurement Assessment Not Made

(e) Media research — Impact Studies on the use of AV programmes (Please indicate the detail of studies taken up, if any) ______

(f) How far integration of media, curriculum and multimedia approach in production has been undertaken by your institute ______

(g) Indicate the steps undertaken by you to integrate AV production, their use from script to telecast/broadcast stage ______

(h) Whether your institute is conducting the pre-telecast and post-telecast activities during and after the viewing/play back of programmes ______ for obtaining the reactions of the target audience __________ Please give details.

(i) How an inbuilt evaluation system to measure the __________ quality of programmes has been developed? __________

(j) What methodologies are being followed __________ by your institution for incorporating research __________ elements in the programmes for effective __________ communication and use __________

(16) Information on EduSat Project

(a) Do you have an EduSat terminal in your organization?

(b) Has it been tested and commissioned?

(c) Are your using it regularly? (Please indicate the time/duration on a weekly basis)

(d) Please state your expenence about EduSat. What suggestions do you propose to improve the utilization of EduSat network?

(e) Are you in a position to create content for EduSat network?

(f) Do you have adequate resource persons in your institute who can deliver on line lecturers/demonstration on the specific content areas.

Suggested Performa for the Formulation of a Research Proposal for an Aspect of Educational Technology

1. Title

The title of the research proposal should be small. It should not be too lengthy and specific to the area of the study.

2. Statement of the Problem

It is not exactly similar as the title of the study. Statement of the problem is the explanation of the title in terms of the scope of the study.

3. Review of Related Literature

A summary of the writings of the authorities and of previous research provides evidence that the researcher is familiar with both is already known and not known. A brief resume and references of related studies found in journals, magazines, abstracts and reports should be made. This ensures that previous research eliminates the risk of duplication of what has been done and provides basis for selecting a problem for research.

4. Significance and Need of the Problem

A research proposal normally specifies how the results and findings of the study can influence educational theory and improve practices. The need and urgency for undertaking a study can be shown in several similar and different ways.

First, a need for a research study is to show the time gap between the earlier study and the present one, and therefore the new knowledge, techniques, or conditions justify the need to replicate the study.

Second, there is need for a study to relate it to the existing social issues and priority areas in the context of national/international educational development.

Thirdly, the need for a study is to show the lack of information about a problem by presenting the supporting statements of other studies.

Lastly, the need to demonstrate that there are gaps in the knowledge provided by previous researchers and to show how the present study will help to fill in these gaps and add to the existing knowledge.

5. Definitions, Assumptions, Limitation and Delimitations

(i) Definitions

In this section, the researcher is required to define all unusual terms that could be misinterpreted. These definitions in operational terms help the researcher to establish a frame of reference with which he/she approaches the problem. The variable named in the title of the study should be defined in operational terms. For example, 'academic achievement' or 'study habit' cannot be used as criteria unless they are defined as observable samples of behaviour. A score on an achievement test is an operational definition of academic achievement. Similarly, grade/rank on a 'Study Habit Inventory' obtained by a child is an operational definition of study habit.

(ii) Assumptions

Assumptions are statements of what the researcher believes to be facts but are not verifiable. For example, a researcher may state the assumption the participants observe in group meeting of "Parent-Teachers

Association" in a school, will establish support with teachers as well as with parents, and will not have a reactive effect on the behaviour to be observed.

(iii) Limitations

Limitations indicate the conditions which are beyond the control of the researcher, and thus may place restrictions on the findings of the study and their applications to other situations. For example, due to some reasons, a research tool could not be assigned randomly to experimental and control groups and some limitations.

(iv) Delimitations

Delimitations denote the scope of the study in terms of the area of operation, size of the sample, nature of the population beyond which the findings of the study are not extended.

6. Objective/Research Questions

The objectives specific to the study are stated keeping in view the variable and nature of the research problems.The researcher must state the specific questions in the operational terms whose answers he/she would like to seek after undertaking the research study. Such questions are helpful to researcher to realize the objectives of the study sucessfully. The objectives are specific and achievable and attainable unlike the aims which may not be achieved and higher at the pedestrial level.

7. The Hypothesis

The hypothesis is precisely defined as a tentative or working, proposition suggested as a solution to a problem. It is a powerful tool in research process to achieve dependable knowledge. Hypothesis is formulated only as the suggested solution to the problem, with the objective that the ensuring study may lead either to its rejection or to its retention. It helps the researcher to locate and identify the variable involved in the study methodological produres/techniques that are to be used in the conduct of the research study.

Hypothesis helps the researcher to relate theory to the observation (deductive-inductive paradigm). On the basis of his experience and his knowledge of behaviour in a school situation, the teacher may attempt to relate the behaviour of students to his/her own, to his/her instructional/ evaluation strategies, to change in school environment/conditions and so on. From these observations, the teacher may inductively formulate a hypothesis to explain such relationships. Relevant to a particular research problem, the research may have different hypothesis, but the soundness of the hypothesis will depend upon the background knowledge that the researcher possesses of the area of investigation.

The formulation of hypothesis depends upon the nature of the research method which a researcher uses in the conduct of the study. The researcher uses hypothesis and theory with data in quantative research whereas in qualitative research approach the researcher employs inductive paradigm for generating new hypothesis from the data collected during field work and the researcher begins by employing genuinely open questions rather than testing theoretically derived hypothesis.

Sometimes it is argued that in action research studies, a researcher is merely interested in the solution of a problem which demands immediate solution and thus he/she has merely to check the validity of facts (past or present) and arrange/analyse them chronologically and logically. Thus, the research may not formulate any hypothesis in such studies. But it may be noted that hypothesis for such type of studies may not be formal hypothesis to be tested. Rather, they are written as explicit statements/ questions that tentatively explain the occurrence of events and conditions.

A good hypothesis has certain characteristics which includes : (i) it should be clearly and precisely stated; (ii) it should be testable; (iii) it should state expected relationship between variables in simple langauge; (iv) it should be limited in scope; and (v) it should be consistent with most known facts.

Research hypothesis are classified in the directional and non-directional types. For example, the "Academic achievement of children in a primary school is positively related to its better infrastructure" is a directional hypothesis; whereas the hypothesis: "The academic achievement of primary school children is related to the infrastructure of the school" is a non-directional hypothesis.

8. Method and Design

In this section, the researcher usually needs to discuss the method which he/she may use in the conduct of the study. It will include whether the researcher may use either qualitative approach, quantitative approach, or both.

The selection and use of sampling method/design will also be discussed. It will take discussion on the choice of a particular sampling method, such as random sampling, stratified random sampling, quota, cluster or judgment sampling, etc.

In order to effect relevant data/evidence, the researcher has to make use of certain testing and non-testing devices/tools/techniques, viz., psychological/educational tests, questionaire, rating scales, schedules, observation, interview. The researcher has to provide the details about the tools and techniques which he/she has to develop or procedure for use in the collection of the data. The techniques of data analysis are also discussed in this section.

9. Time Schedule

The researcher should prepare a realistic time schedule for the completion of the study. He/she should mention the time periods which will be utilized in the preliminary preparation field work/data collection, analysis of the data and report writing.

10. Budget Schedule

The research proposal which are submitted to government agencies/ private/autonomous organizations for financial help must furnish the details of the finances which are required by the researcher forthe conduct of the study.

11. Bibliography

The researcher is expected to give a list of the document/research papers, etc. which he/she has consulted in the preparation of the purpose.

Let us illustrate the format of a research proposal for action research with the help of following examples:

Title ______________________________

____

Introduction ______________________________

____

Need and Relevance ______________________________

____

Objectives____________________

Action hypotheses____________________

Methodology

Sample____________________

Tool____________________

Statistical Techniques____________________

Procedure____________________

Analysis and Interpretation____________________

Implication____________________

Conclusion____________________

Most Popular Terms Used/Introduced

Concepts, Hypotheses and Variables

Applied Research	:	Research designed to produce knowledge useful in relating world condition or situation.
Empirical Research	:	Research based on actual, objective, observation of phenomena.
Pure, theoretical or recreational research	:	Research designed to satisfy one's intellectual curiosity about some phenomena.
Deduction	:	A process of reasoning from a theory to specific observations.
Induction	:	A process of reasoning from specific observations to general principles.
Explanation	:	A statement that provides a reason for a phenomena.
General	:	Applicable to many rather than a few cases.
Normative knowledge	:	Evaluation concerned with prescribing what ought to be.
Prediction	:	The application of explanation to events a future. The ability to anticipate future events (correctly)
Probabilistic	:	That does not explain or predict events with 100% accurately.
Provisional	:	Subject to revision and change.
Theory	:	A statement of series of statements that organise, explain and predict knowledge.

Antecedent variable	:	An independent variable that precedes other independent variables.
Arrow diagram	:	A pictorial representation of a research is explanatory scheme.
Casual hypothesis	:	A hypothesis in which the independent variable is considered to be the cause of the dependent variable.
Concept	:	The definition or meaning of a phenomenon used in empirical research.
Correlative hypothesis	:	A hypothesis that proposes a relationship between two variables without indicating any relationship.
Curvilinear relationship	:	A relationship between two variables that may be described by a curved rather than a straight line.
Dependable variable	:	The phenomena thought to be influenced, affected or caused by some other phenomena.
Direct relationship	:	A relationship in which the values of one variable increase as the values of another variable increase.
Directional hypothesis	:	A hypothesis that specifies the expected relationship between two or more variables.
Hypothesis	:	A statement proposing a relationship between two or more variables.
Independent variable	:	The phenomena thought to influence, or cause some other phenomena.

Intervening variable	:	A variable between independent and dependent variable.
Inverse relationship	:	A relationship in which the values of one variable increases as the values of another variable decrease.
Logarithmic relationship	:	A mathematical relationship in which increasing amounts of one variable have less effect an another variable.
Extraneous factors	:	Other factors besides independent variables that may cause change in dependent variable.
Factorial Design	:	Experimental design used to measure effect of two or more independent variables and in combination.
Field Experiments	:	Experimental designs applied in a natural setting.
Frequency Distribution Control	:	When frequency distribution of a characteristic is the same in the experimental groups as in control group.
Instrument decay	:	Change in measurement device used to measure dependent variable producing changes.
Internal Validity	:	The ability to show that manipulation of independent variable causes the dependent variable to change.
Non-experimental design	:	Research design characterised by presence of single group or lack of control over assignment of subjects to control and experimental groups.

Pre test	:	Measurement of dependent variables prior to administration of treatment or manipulation of independent variables.
Post test	:	Measurement of dependent variables after manipulation of independent variable.
Research design	:	A plan specifying how the researcher intends to fulfil the goals of study; a logical plan to test the hypothesis.
Statistical regression	:	Change in dependent variable due to' temporary nature of extreme values.
Test stimulus	:	The independent variable.
Testing	:	Effects of pre test on dependent variable.

Sampling

Cluster sample	:	A probability sample used when no list of elements exist.
Element	:	Unit of analysis or entity about which information is collected.
Sample	:	Is a subset of all the observations covered by the hypothesis.
Sampling fraction	:	The proportion of the population included in the sample.
Simple Random Sample	:	A probability sample in which each element has an equal chance of being selected.
Stratified sample	:	A probability sample in which elements showing one or more characteristics are grouped and elements are selected from each

group in proportion to their representation.

Survey Research and Interviewing - Types of Data and their Collection

Ambiguous question	:	A question containingj a concept not clearly defined.
Closed ended question	:	A question with response alternatives provided.
Document analysis	:	Data collection based on records kept by individuals or institutions.
Double barred question	:	A question that is really two questions in one.
Interview data	:	Observation derived from written or verbal questioning.
Open ended question	:	A question with no response alternatives.
Randomized response technique (RRT)	:	A method of obtaining accurate answers to sensitive questions that protects respondent's privacy.
Y Intercept	:	The value of Y (dependent variable) in a regression equation when the value of X (independent variable) is 0.
Multivariate data analysis	:	Data analysis technique designed to test hypothesis involving more than two variables.
Spurious relationship	:	A relationship between two variables caused entirely by the impact of a third.
Two-way analysis of variables	:	An extension of the analysis of variance procedure to allow controlling for a third variable.

Survey instrument	:	Schedule of questions to be asked of respondent.
Survey research	:	Survey based on interview method of data collection.
Accretion measures	:	Indirect observation of the accumulation of materials.
Covert observations	:	The observer's purpose is kept secret from those being observed.
Ethnography	:	Participant observation in a natural setting.
Overt observation	:	Those being observed are informed of the observer's pressure and purpose.
Structured observation	:	Systematic observation and recording of the incidence of specific behaviours.
Unstructured observation	:	Observation in which all behaviour and activities are recorded.
Bar graph	:	A type of graphic display of frequency or % distribution of data.
Central tendency	:	The most frequent, common or central value in the distribution of values of a variable.
Descriptive statistic	:	Math summary of measurements for one variable.
Dispersion	:	The distribution of data values around the most common, middle or central value.
Frequency curve	:	A line graph indicating frequency distribution.

Histogram	:	The type of bar graph used to depict interval and ratio level measures.
Interquartile range	:	The middle 50% of observations.
Mean	:	The sum of values of a variable divided by the number of values.
Mean deviation	:	A measure of dispersion of data points for interval and ratio level data.
Median	:	The category or value above and below which 1/2 of observations lie.
Mode	:	The category with the greatest frequency of obsetvations.
Negatively showed	:	Distribution of values in which more observations lie to the left of the middle value.
Pie graph	:	Graphic display of frequency distribution.
Range	:	The distance between highest and lowest values into which observations fall.
Standard deviation	:	The measure of dispersion of data points about the mean interval and ratio level data.
Standard error	:	The standard deviation of sample means about the mean of sample means.
Univariate - data analysis	:	Analysis of a single variable.
Z score	:	The number of standard deviation that a score deviated from the mean score.

Analysis of variance :	A technique for measuring the relationship between one nominal or ordinal variable and one interval level variable.
Chi-square :	A measure used with cross tabulation to determine if the relationship is statistically significant.
Correlation matrix :	A table showing the correlation among a number of variables.
F ratio :	A measure used with the analysis of variance to determine if a relationship is statistically significant.
Negative relationship :	When high values of one variable are associated with low values of another variable.
Regression relationship :	A technique for measuring the relationship between two interval variable have less effect on another variable.
Null hypothesis :	A hypothesis that proposes non-relationship between two variables.
Tantology :	A hypothesis in which the independent and the dependent variables are identical, making it impossible to disconfirm.
Unit of analysis :	The type of individual, group or institution specified in a researcher's hypothesis.
Construct validity :	Demonstrating validity for a measure by showing that it is related to the measure of another concept.

Content validity	:	Demonstrating that the full domain of a concept is measured.
Guttman scale	:	A multiple measure in which respondents are presented with increased difficult measures for an attitude.
Index	:	A multiple measure in which individual scores on a set of items are combined to form a summary measure.
Level of measurement	:	An indication of what is meant by assigning score or numerals to empirical observations.
Operational definition	:	The rules by which concept is measured and scores assigned.
Ratio	:	A measure for which the scores possess the full mathematical properties of the numbers.
Reliability	:	The extent to which measure yields the same results on repeated trials.
Test-retest	:	Calculating reliability by repeating the same measure at two or more points in time.
Thurstone scale	:	A multi-item measure with the objective to select items that represent the entire range of an attitude at equal intervals.
Validity	:	The correspondence between a measure and the concept, it is supposed to measure.

Research Designs

Assignment at random	:	Random assignment of subjects to experimental and control groups.

Case study design	:	In-depth study of a single case or several cases. It is also called non-experimental design in which the investigator has little or no control over events.
Classic experimental design	:	Experiment with random assignment of subjects to experimental and control groups with pre test and post test for both groups.
Control group	:	A group of subjects that does not receive the treatment or test stimulus.
Cross sectional design	:	Research design in which the measures of independent and dependent variables are taken at the same time.
Deviant case study	:	Study of a case that deviates from other cases.
Experimental group	:	A group of subjects receiving treatment or test stimulus.
Experimental mortality	:	A differential loss of subjects from experimental and control groups that affects equivalency of groups.
Experimentation	:	Research using an experimental research design in which the researcher has control over the independent variables, the units of analysis of their environments.
External Validity	:	The ability to generalise from one set of research findings to other situations.

□

14

BIBLIOGRAPHY

Aghi, M.B. (1977) Imact of Educational Programes Through Site for Rajasthan Children: Concept Publishing Co., N. Delhi.

Agrawal, B.C. (1998) T.V. Comes to Villages : An Evaluation of Satelite Instructional Television Experiment : Report by Development Education and Communication Unit, Space Application Centre, Ahmedbad.

Agrawal, B.C., Karnik Kiran And Others (1999) Children Television in India; A Situation Analysis; N. Delhi: Concept Publishing Co.

All India Association For Educational Technology Educational Technology Potent but Ignored : Publisher W. News Magazine Vol; No. 8.

Bafile, C. (1998) Technology Gets Real with Multimedia Prose Edu World; Published by Classroom Connect

Baggaley, G. (1986) Formative Evaluation of ETV- *Jounal of Educational Communication*; Canada.

Behera, S.C. (1991) Impact of ETV on the Competency of Elementary School Teachers in "Media and Technology for Human Resource Development" Journal NDE.

Biswal, B.N. (1979) A Study of Correspondence Education in India- Ph.d. thesis in MS University of Baroda.

Chaudhari, M.M. (1986) Media Education and Development Published by NCERT, New Delhi 110006.

Chaudhary, S.V.S. (2009) Towards a Culture of ICT. Enabled Education; Published by IGNOU, New Delhi 110068.

DECU, ISRO (1984) ISRO-UGC Workshop on VI and Tecnology Education.

DECU, ISRO (1995) An Insat Effect Study ISRO Ahemdabad.

DECU, ISRO (1984) International Workshop on the use of Video for Education (Formative Research).

Educational Media (2008) World Conference on the Educational Multimedia Hypermedia and Tele Communications; Jan. 2008. Aace.

Fieldman, T. (1991) Multimedia in the 1990; Heat Publication; London.

Goel, D.R. & Earnest (2006) Media and ICT in Education — National Seminar on Educational Technology, NCERT, N. Delhi, A Report Paper.

Gokul, S. (2005) Multimedia Magic, BPB Publishers, C.F., N. Delhi,

Goodwin, M. (1995) Making Multimedia Work, a Division of Pustak Mahal, N. Delhi.

Hiltz. Sr. (1994) The Virtual Classroom: Learning Without Limit via Computer Networks; Norwood: Arlex Publishing Corporation, New York (USA).

Harmesh Lal (2010) Paper on Perspectives in ET. Vasunandi Publication, Meerut

Harmesh Lal (2011) Manual of Low Cost Technological Aids; Published by Sai Publication; Jain Colony, Ballabhgarh-121004

Indira Gandhi National Open University, New Delhi (1998) Using Satelite Technology for Special Orientation of Primary Teachers in MP-Published in Indian Journal of Open Learning.

Indira Gandhi National Open University, New Delhi (2000) Media Education with Special Reference to Educational T.V. By Prof. Harmeshlal. Published in Staff and EDL, Development International : Vol 4, No. 3.

Indira Gandhi National Open University, New Delhi (2008) Courseware Development Process-2-MES-034

John V. and M.M. (1998) Multimedia Production Planning and Delivery by Mcmillan Computer Pub, ND.

Johnson, G.B. and Goslynra (1989) Political Science Research Methods Published by Prenticahall of India Pvt. Ltd., New Delhi.

Janet, B.I. (1989) — Science Research Methods, Prentica Hall, New Delhi.

Keith, F. Punch (2009) — Intoduction to Research Methods by Sage Publication, New Delhi.

Kota Open University Kota (Rajasthan) (1996) — Study Materials in EDL Technology for Med. 06 (Pt. II) Modules.

Kumar, Meenu (2009) — Teaching of English Through Multimedia; Ph.D. Thesis; MD University, Rothak

Lindsay, P.H. Norman, D.A. (1977) — Human Information Processing Published by Academic Press, New York.

Mohanty, L. and Vohra, N. (2006) — ICT Strategies for Schools; New Delhi, Sage Publications.

Mahapatra, B.C. (2005) — Information Technology and Education with Special Reference to Importance of Computer in Classroom by Sarup Publication, New Delhi.

Marsh. M. (2007) — Using Multimedia Effectively in the Teaching-Learning Process; Worcester Country School, Berlin.

Ministry of Human Resource Development (MHRD) (2004) — Educational Software for Edusat Complied by Prof. Harmesh Lal

Ministry of Human Resource Development (MHRD) (1986) — National Policy on Education 1986 and POA, 1992.

MHRD, Govt. of India (2012) — National Policy on ICT in School Education.

MHRD, Govt. of India (1966) — Educaton and National Development; Report of

Education Commission (1964-66) New Delhi.

MHRD, Govt. of India (1977) Satellite Instructional TV Experiment in Orissa by Saulat Rahman.

National Council for Science and Technology Communication, New Delhi (1991) Pump from the Dump by Arvind Gupta.

National Council for Science and technology Communication, New Delhi (1991) Leaf Zoo by Arvind Gupta.

National Book Trust New Delhi (2006) Ten Little Fingers by Arvind Gupta.

National Book Trust New Delhi (1999) Shikshan Sahayak Samagari by Meri Ain Das Gupta.

National Council of Educational Search and Training, New Delhi-110016 (1982) Manaul of Low Cost Teaching Aids.

(1999) NCERT, Delhi Teaching Aids in Mathematics at Middle and High School Level.

(1995) NCERT, Delhi Mathematic Club Activities.

(1982) NCERT, Delhi UNESCO Case Study on Low Cost Teaching Aids.

(1977) NCERT, Delhi Workshop on Low Cost Teaching Aids at Ban Khedi (MP)- A Report.

(1983) NCERT, Delhi Development of Science Equipment from Local Resources for Teaching Science at Elementary Level.

(2006) NCERT, Delhi National Curriculum Framework; Position Paper on Educational Technlogy.

(1997) NCERT, Delhi Development Learning-Material for Literacy and Continuing Education.

(2003) NCERT, Delhi Quality Education TV Programmes for Children Published in *Primary Teacher* Vol XXVIII; No. 2.

(1982) NCERT, Delhi Low Cost Teaching Aids for Rural Primary School in *Primary Teacher* Vol 7; No. 2.

(2000) NCERT, Delhi Special Issue on Curriculum Development II Published in Journal of Indian Education Vol. XXV….

(2001) NCERT, Delhi National Policies on Education Since 1911 Published in *Primary Teacher,* Vol. XXVI-No. 4.

NCERT (2006) National Seminar on Perspectives of ET – A Report.

NCERT (1989) Inservice Teacher Education for Primary School Teachers — A Package.

NCERT (2000) Television, the Pied Piper of the Century.

NCERT (1991) Using RCCP and TV in Classroom.

NCERT (1978) Report of the Working Group on Educational Technology.

NCERT (2005) National Curriculum Framework. A Document.

NCERT (1993) Project Evaluation Report on Classroom 2000+.

NCERT (2003) — An Impact Evaluation Study of the Centrally Sponsored Scheme of Educational Technology.

National Institute of Open Schooling, Noida (2002) — Interactive Video Technology Published in *OSAC Journal*; Vol. I, No. 1.

(2003) — Why my Child should Watch ETV Programme: Published in *OSAC Journal* Vol. III; No. 1.

(2009) — Effect of Teaching Learning Through Edusat on Academic Performance of Children: Published in *OSAC Journal*, Vol. VII, No. 182.

(2011) — Role of Media and Technology by Kiran Karnik in *Comosa Journal of Open Schooling*.

Passi, B.K. (2000) — Formative Research for Video Production - A Seminar Report; IGNOU-UNESCO Chair.

Rajasthan State Study Book Mandal, Jaipur (2014) — Preservice Teacher Training Material on ICT by State Institute of Educational Research and Training, Udaipur

Rajput, J.S. and Walia (2002) — Teacher Education in India; New Delhi, Sterling Publishers Pvt. Ltd.

Romiszowski, A.J. (1991) — Selection and Use of Instructional Media; Kogan Page Ltd., London

Ruhela, S.P. (2002) — The Roots of Educational Technology Published by Indian Publishers and Distributers, New Delhi (Edited by Paul Saettler).

Schramm, V. (1977)	Big Media Little Media; Beverly Hills Published by C.A. Sage, New Delhi.
Senapati, H.K. (2004)	Integrating Digital Technology into Constructivist Learning Environment (Paper Presented in International Conference at Saurastra University, Rajkot).
Singh, L.C. (2010)	Educational Technology Vasunand Publication, Meerut
Singh, R.P. and Rana, G. (2004)	Teaching Strategies; APH Publishing Corporation; New Delhi.
Spence R (2001)	Information Visualisation; Addison, Weslay, Boston; USA
UNESCO	ICT in Education – a Curriculumn for Schools and Programme for Teacher Development http.11 Portal unesco.org.
UNESCO Regional Office for Education in Asia and The pacific; Bangkok (1982)	Low Cost Educational Materials (APEID) – A Report
UNESCO Regional Office for Education in Asia and The Pacific; Bangkok (1980)	Low Cost Educational Materials How to Make; How to Use; and How to Adopt-Vol. I.
Unicef, 73 Lodhi Estate New Delhi (1987)	Preparation for Understanding by Keith Waren.

□□□